THE WORST **TV** SHOWS EVER

THE

WORST TV SHOWS

EVER

**Those TV Turkeys We Will Never Forget . . .
(No Matter How Hard We Try)**

BART ANDREWS
with
BRAD DUNNING

Foreword by Cleveland Amory

A Dutton Paperback
E.P. DUTTON
NEW YORK

For
CHUCK BARRIS,
wunderkind
of the wasteland

For information contact: E.P. Dutton, 2 Park Avenue, New York, N.Y. 10016

Library of Congress Cataloging in Publication Data
Andrews, Bart.   The worst TV shows ever.
Includes index.
1. Television programs—United States.   2. Television broadcasting—United States—Anecdotes, facetiae, satire, etc.   I. Dunning, Brad, joint author.   II. Title.
PN1992.3.U5A5   791.45'7   79-24207

ISBN: 0-525-47592-3

Published simultaneously in Canada by Clarke, Irwin & Company Limited, Toronto and Vancouver

Designed by Barbara Huntley

10   9   8   7   6   5   4   3   2   1

First Edition

CONTENTS

FOREWORD
by Cleveland Amory

In my thirteen years as chief critic for *TV Guide,* there were many memorable moments, not the least of which was the time Mr. Michael Dann, then vice president in charge of programming for CBS, delivered a truly earthshaking pronouncement. "The biggest crisis facing the TV networks," he said, "is that they are running out of old movies."

As Mr. Dann's audience sat stunned, I remember thinking that this was a time for calm. And, when it came my turn to speak to the issue, I suggested that the American public had taken terrible blows before—and yet we had always measured up. I asked that we think back for a moment—to New York's blackout of '65, to the blizzard of '88, to the burning of Washington and Valley Forge. I suggested that before we watched our next old movie, in the privacy of our own homes, we could ask ourselves, "Is this movie really necessary?" And the next time we felt we just *had* to have a movie, we could call Movie Anonymous, who would send somebody to sit with us in that terribly difficult prime time.

You can follow a similar strategy in order to break the "bad TV" habit—to wean yourself from some of those awful TV shows, such as those discussed in this book.

Another milestone in the history of "TV criticism" was reached by Representative Roman Pucinski of Illinois. The noble Roman was making a speech before the House of Representatives on the ticklish subject of whether or not TV news was fair—and he thought it was not.

Television, he said, had an important role in moving products from the factory to the American home. "If people lose faith in TV news," he declared, "how long will it be before they lose faith in TV advertising?" Imagine! The very thought that the truth of TV advertising could be denied strikes a mortal blow at the foundation of the industry. Picture what could result if we really doubted that Brut was what made Joe Namath able to face the day, that O.J. Simpson really didn't run for daylight through airports, or that Pelé wouldn't leave home without his American Express card.

Advertisers, after all, put down a lot of money to produce the turkeys you'll soon be reading about here. And ask yourself what kind of a world would it be if we doubted *The Baileys of Balboa*, *Me and the Chimp*, or *My Mother, the Car*—or for that matter, my own show, *O.K. Crackerby*, which is also mentioned here? (Imagine Bart Andrews using a show of mine as one of the worst! The man is incorrigible.)

I remember especially vividly a piece of news about television that came out of Nashville, Tennessee. It was a story about a lady named Rosalie Sneyd. Mrs. Sneyd, it seemed, got so tired of her husband's watching football on television that she put an advertisement in the paper. "For Sale," the advertisement read, "Husband and TV Set."

The response was gratifying. One woman lauded Mrs. Sneyd to the skies—particularly for her refusal of the first offer she received—$200. "I think," she said, "he's worth more than that. The TV set is only black and white, but my husband is quite colorful." Another woman thought $250 might be a fairer price, and went on to break it down to $200 for the husband and $50 for the set. I couldn't help agreeing with her. After all, even if one felt only so-so about the husband, $50 for a working set was pretty good—and the set must have been working or why all the fuss in the first place?

The late, great Fred Allen once said that the average age of the American public was twelve—and he added that "the average man was well below the average." As *The Worst TV Shows Ever* amply demonstrates, the TV networks have for years been going on Mr. Allen's belief. And author Bart Andrews quotes H. L. Mencken's dictum, "Nobody ever went broke underestimating the taste of the American public."

Mencken was, alas, right. Most of the perpetrators of these shows did not go broke, and a lot of them are unfortunately still operating. A few are millionaires. But we can take heart that some did lose money on these fiascos; that should give us, if not satisfaction, at least hope.

PREFACE

We've watched a *lot* of television. In fact, more than half a century of combined viewing by two confirmed TV addicts has made this book possible. And it hasn't been easy. For every *I Love Lucy* and *Upstairs, Downstairs,* there have been six *Gilligan's Islands* and a dozen *Lost in Spaces*—and we have the astigmatism to prove it!

Given this vast wasteland, how did we go about compiling a book about lousy television shows? With some 3,500 programs from which to choose, the task of boiling them down to a manageable number of all-time stinkers was a real challenge, much like trying to catalog the grains of sand on a beach.

We decided first to concentrate mainly on shows telecast in prime time, although we included such daytime disasters as *Queen For a Day* and *Supermarket Sweep,* a particularly dreadful pair of potboilers that, thank God, have long been banished to TV's Boot Hill. We have not included any soap operas on our "worst" list for a good reason: We hate them all. But to make up for this shortcoming, we have added *The Survivors* and *Beacon Hill,* two prime-time dramas that turned out to be 99 44/100 percent pure Oxydol.

Sitcoms were our greatest target, not because they were worse than other categories of shows, but because there have been more of them through TV history. Except for a brief period in the late 1950s when westerns were riding high, situation comedy has always been the major force in television. And, speaking of westerns, only *The Dakotas* is in our book. This horsey little monstrosity was really no worse than a few dozen other oaters that once rode the TV range—*Tate, Whispering Smith, ad nauseum*—but we didn't want to subject the reader to more than one, so why not *Dakotas*? Chad Everett won't mind much; he hated it, too, and he was the star!

We especially enjoyed writing about the really classic clinkers—those shows that lasted only a few weeks, such as, *The Tammy Grimes Show, The Big Party,* and *The Jerry Lewis Show.* (Two bombs actually had their opening *and* closing nights on the same day! You'll have to read our book to find out which ones—unless, of course, you're a TV addict yourself.)

Then there were the *popular* bombs. TV-land has been fairly littered with them since 1947—shows that have ridden mediocrity to great success, like *Gilligan's Island, Hogan's Heroes, The Newlywed Game, Hee Haw,* and others. These are particularly disturbing because they suggest that at times the public will settle for *anything* in the way of entertainment, even patent drivel.

We should inform you that our choices are purely personal. We used no formal barometer, only our own senses of what's rotten on the tube. Perhaps you won't agree with a number of our selections—and surely you'll have your own pet turkeys. But you're sure to go along with such inane creations as *My Mother, the Car*—the classic "worst TV show ever"—and *Me and the Chimp,* a runner-up for the dubious title.

We should add that we intend no malice toward those who gave their best for our worst. After all, it's not entirely fair to dismiss the efforts of hundreds of dedicated technicians and performers just because the end result was a failure. As Fred Silverman said in early 1979 when addressing a large contingent of Hollywood producers and writers: "The road to *The Gong Show* is paved with good intentions."

Rather, we wrote this book so that we and our readers could have some fun remembering TV's low spots. We hope you will enjoy our efforts to share with you TV's worst moments, and trust you will not abide by the old adage that a book is only as good as its subject matter.

ACKNOWLEDGMENTS

Thank you—the library staff at the Academy of Motion Picture Arts and Sciences; Thomas J. Watson of CBS-TV; Marco DeLeon, Jr.; Howard Frank (Personality Photos, Inc., Box 50, Midwood Station, Brooklyn, New York 11230; catalog available upon request) for the matchless photo collection; and Bill Whitehead who, once again, endured the agonies of another Bart Andrews book.

THE WORST
TV
SHOWS EVER

THE BAILEYS OF BALBOA

THE GUILTY PARTIES

Executive Producer:	Keefe Brasselle
Producer/Director:	Bob Sweeney
Director:	Gary Nelson, et al.
Writer:	Richard Powell, et al.
Cameraman:	Neal Beckner
Film Editor:	Alan Jaggs

A Richelieu Production in association with the CBS Television Network for CBS-TV.

Starring Paul Ford as Sam Bailey, Sterling Holloway as Buck Singleton, Les Brown, Jr. as Jim Bailey, Clint Howard as Stanley, John Dehner as Cecil Wyntoon, and Judy Carne as Barbara Wyntoon.

Debuted Thursday, September 24, 1964, 9:30 P.M. E.D.T. on CBS-TV.

THE FORMAT

Sam Bailey (Paul Ford) is the owner-operator of Bailey's Landing, a rundown marina located in the exclusive boating community of Balboa, California, an hour down the coast from Los Angeles. With his son Jim (Les Brown, Jr.) and first (and only) mate Buck Singleton (Sterling Holloway), the widower takes out fishing parties and conducts harbor excursions in his ancient craft, *The Island Princess*.

Bailey's escapades are anathema to the highfalutin' boating fraternity who constitute his neighbors. As Paul Ford described his character: "Bailey docks his dilapidated boat next to their fancy yacht club. The socially prominent members of the club spearhead all sorts of campaigns to get me out of their midst, but I've been there longer than they have."

Commodore Cecil Wyntoon (John Dehner) heads the contingent bent on removing Bailey and his blight from Balboa. His job becomes more difficult when he discovers that his beautiful young daughter, Barbara (Judy Carne), has fallen in love with Sam's son, Jim. What ensues is a family rivalry reminiscent of the Montagues and Capulets, but without even a trace of Shakespeare's genius.

Week after week, it's Bailey trying to top Wyntoon, Wyntoon trying to outdo Bailey. A good-natured tug-of-war between the common folk and the society set has worked well for other TV shows—most notably *The Beverly Hillbillies*—but *Baileys* relied too heavily on the one-joke premise, and the writers, uninspired by the program blueprints afforded them, did nothing to enliven the drab proceedings. The characterizations were shallow and uninteresting, and even the considerable talents of Paul Ford, Sterling Holloway, and John Dehner could not make this sow's ear sitcom into a silk purse program.

In television, this happens all the time. It's called a flop.

MEMORABLE MOMENTS

- An argument over which late-night movie to watch leads Buck to leave the marina.
- Sam's quite pleased with his catch: a city slicker who wants to charter *The Island Princess*.
- Buck unwittingly buys a "hot" holiday turkey.

SOME KIND WORDS FROM ...

Rex Polier of the *Philadelphia Bulletin*:
"Typical soupy sentimental Hollywood situation comedy."

John Horn of the *New York Herald Tribune*:
"Had to be seen not to be believed."

Jack E. Anderson of the *Miami Herald*:
"So flat, it's one of the season's expendable shows."

The darkly handsome actor Keefe Brasselle, one-time go-fer for CBS's "Smiling Cobra," Jim Aubrey, was the executive producer of *The Baileys of Balboa*, one of the three series his Richelieu Productions company sold to the network for the 1964–65 season. Brasselle's questionable relationship with Aubrey caused the CBS chieftain's downfall in 1965.

Character actor Sterling Holloway played the tangle-footed, dim-witted Buck Singleton—first and only mate aboard Bailey's *Island Princess* charter boat. For years Holloway played Waldo Binney on William Bendix's *Life of Riley* series.

The cast of *The Baileys of Balboa*. Seated are producer/director Bob Sweeney and young Clint Howard (brother of Ronny Howard) with Sterling Holloway. Standing (*l. to r.*) are Paul Ford, Les Brown, Jr., Judy Carne, and John Dehner.

A scene from the premiere episode of *The Baileys of Balboa.* Series star Paul Ford is pictured here with Rosemary DeCamp, who played Clint Howard's grandmother. Ford is determined to find out what sort of bait the kid is using to catch all the white sea bass.

On location in Balboa, California, a boating community near Newport Beach. (*l. to r.*) Sterling Holloway, Paul Ford, and Bob Sweeney who is explaining the fine art of comedy acting to two veterans who don't appear to be very happy about being in this turkey.

THE BUSINESS BEHIND THE BOX

"I am the most confident man in the world," announced Keefe Brasselle, the arrogant young assistant to the president of the CBS television network, James T. Aubrey. "I have three shows on the air this year. Next year, I'll have five. None of them will fail."

Brasselle, a one-time nightclub performer who dubbed himself "Mr. Fabulous," was talking to Cecil Smith of the *Los Angeles Times* a few days before the start of the 1964–65 season. His newly formed company, Richelieu Productions, had managed to sell three series to the number one network its first time out: *The Reporter*, a drama set in a New York City newsroom starring Harry Guardino; *The Cara Williams Show*, a half-hour sitcom starring the comedienne and Frank Aletter; and *The Baileys of Balboa*, another situation comedy with Paul Ford in the lead.

No "Sammy" had ever run so fast or climbed so high so suddenly as Brasselle. His corporate mentor, Jim Aubrey, had reached his own apogee of power at CBS as the year 1964 approached—he was responsible for bringing in $40 million a year in advertising revenue to the network. *Baileys* actually was born out of Aubrey's discontent over the premise for *Gilligan's Island*, a sitcom scheduled to run on the network in the fall of 1964. He could not see how producer Sherwood Schwartz could sustain a show set on a desert island. "I want a charter boat to take people to different places," said Aubrey to a bewildered Schwartz, who refused to alter his original concept. Aubrey, who built his reputation on cold formula—the hell with quality, programs either score high ratings or drop out—went ahead and authorized another program—one about a charter boat service. And it just so happened that Aubrey's buddy Brasselle had an idea for such a show.

By March 1964, CBS had negotiated an unprecedented contract with Brasselle's fledgling concern—it had given the green light to not only *Baileys*, but also Cara Williams' sitcom and *The Reporter*—all without pilots, only scripts. Brasselle, once well known in the industry as Aubrey's go-fer, was now a big-shot producer. He went out and signed actor Paul Ford, late of the *Bilko* series and at the time starring in the Broadway smash comedy, *Never Too Late*, to head the cast of *The Baileys of Balboa*. Ford was a long-time series holdout, having exited TV when the Phil Silvers comedy left the air in 1959. It was considered something of a coup to capture the actor for any show.

Before the series had even one foot of film in the can, the FCC was on the production company's back. Were there, as the government contended, conflicting interests and hidden partnerships masking the Richelieu production firm? There were even rumors that Aubrey was getting sizable kickbacks in the form of free limousines and a padded expense account from Brasselle's company. Aubrey was in considerable hot water and no one could extricate him from this bath of discontent. There was nothing left to do but wait it out while the FCC investigated the alleged wrongdoings.

Production on *Baileys* began in the late spring of 1964 in anticipation of a fall premiere. Bob Sweeney, a former actor, was signed to produce and direct the series. Brasselle retained the title of executive producer although he spent most of his time supervising *The Reporter* in New York.

Production difficulties arose immediately. The show was set in Balboa, California, a seashore community inhabited mostly by boat-loving folks, but the real folks of Balboa didn't want the TV crews invading their tranquil marinas, and it took considerable persuading to allow even a few days of location filming. It became necessary for the company to travel to Balboa every six weeks, erect anew an entire outdoor set and afterwards completely tear it down, just to shoot the exteriors for a half-dozen segments. By the time they realized their mistake, it was too late to change the show to *The Baileys of Santa Monica* or . . . *Pismo Beach*.

By the time the first thirteen segments were completed, star Ford was having second thoughts. He missed New York, where he had spent the majority of his professional career. He had yet to get his sea legs and his role of Sam Bailey was that of an old salt, a rugged individualist seaman of the old school. "Never even been on a boat, except the Staten Island Ferry," Ford remarked during a summer 1964 newspaper interview. "But then again I was never in the Army but I played a colonel on *Bilko* and another one in *Teahouse of the August Moon*, which shows you can learn anything. Acting is just imagination." It was this urge not to be stereotyped that led Ford to accept the *Baileys'* role. "I have to be flexible," he noted.

The show was pitted against the top-rated *Peyton Place* which had debuted only a week earlier, but had quickly won the lion's share of the available audience. It was an uphill climb for Bailey and his brigade, but they never succeeded in getting out of Nielsen's ratings cellar. By February, it was clear that the series' showing would never improve. For the season, *Bailey* ranked 91 out of 117 shows, including even the nightly network news programs (everything telecast from 6 to 11 P.M.). With a 13.0 rating (and a 21 share of the audience), *Baileys* sank into oblivion. Along with it went Keefe Brasselle's other two series, *The Reporter* and *The Cara Williams Show* . . . and Brasselle's two new limousines, his new Manhattan townhouse, yacht. . . .

When the smoke from the wreckage cleared, it was not only Brasselle who lost his shirt, but also his mentor Jim Aubrey, who was unceremoniously dethroned as president of the network by William Paley, Chairman of the Board of CBS, in late February 1965.

"My shows had nothing to do with Aubrey's demise," claims former producer Brasselle. "It was office politics, and nothing more."

BEACON HILL

THE GUILTY PARTIES

Executive Producer:	Beryl Vertue
Producer:	Jacqueline Babbin
Directors:	Fielder Cook, Peter Lewis, Jay Sandrich, Mel Ferber
Head Writer:	Sidney Carroll
Costume Designer:	Joseph G. Aulisi
Set Decorator:	John Wendell
Art Director:	Thomas H. John
Music by:	Marvin Hamlisch
Casting:	Juliet Taylor

A Robert Stigwood Organization production for CBS-TV.

Starring Roy Cooper as Trevor Bullock, David Dukes as Robert Lassiter, Stephen Elliott as Benjamin Lassiter, Edward Herrmann as Richard Palmer, Nancy Marchand as Mary Lassiter, Maeve McGuire as Maude Palmer, Deann Mears as Emily Bullock, Michael Nouri as Giorgio Bellonci, Linda Purl as Betsy Bullock, George Rose as Arthur Hacker, David Rounds as Terence O'Hara, Paul Rudd as Brian Mallory, Barry Snider as Harry Emmet, Beatrice Straight as Emmeline Hacker, Sydney Swire as Eleanor, Holland Taylor as Marilyn Gardiner, Kathryn Walker as Fawn Lassiter, Richard Ward as William Piper, and Kitty Winn as Rosamond Lassiter.

Debuted Monday, August 25, 1975, 9 P.M. E.D.T. on CBS-TV.

THE FORMAT

"Catch the Brightest Stars on CBS," was the network's 1975 battle cry, the slogan designed to woo potential viewers away from NBC and ABC. Among these "bright" new stellar attractions was *Beacon Hill*, a soapy concoction based (very) loosely on *Upstairs, Downstairs.*

Like the Bellamys of Eaton Place, the Lassiters of Beacon Hill enjoy all the trappings of wealth without ever quite noticing that it is their servants who really rule the roost. Ben Lassiter (Stephen Elliott), the powerful patriarch of this Boston family, is a hard-driving industrialist and political boss who is first-generation Irish-American. He has worked his way through law school, married his wife Mary (Nancy Marchand), and together they have become the parents of four daughters and one son.

Son Robert (David Dukes) has lost his arm in the war and spends much of his time moping about the mansion, his hair slicked back like Valentino, the idol of the day (the show is set in the 1920s). In the opener, father has come to fetch junior from the scandal and ruin of a Negro cathouse. Fawn Lassiter (Kathryn Walker) is the "free-spirited" offspring, the Bohemian through whose eyes we take a look at the arts of the 1920s. Modeled loosely after Zelda Fitzgerald, Fawn drinks too much, strips at parties, and lives with poets. She even submits to a screen test for the emerging U.S. film industry.

There's Emily Bullock (DeAnn Mears) who has discovered alcohol, Maude Palmer (Maeve McGuire) who has married into a thoroughbred family, and Rosamond Lassiter (Kitty Winn), who is plain and unmarried. There is a lot of talk of sex, so much so that Richard Schickel of *Time* concluded: "The Lassiters are a bunch of sex maniacs."

The household staff, directed by the head butler Arthur Hacker (George Rose), has its own set of problems, and their lives, as one might suspect, are totally enmeshed with those of their employers. His wife Emmeline Hacker (Beatrice Straight) is something of a heartless slave-driver, having none of the sympathetic qualities that endeared the character of Mrs. Hudson in *Upstairs, Downstairs.*

Upstairs, Downstairs was a charming, well-done, superior program, something to be treasured and remembered fondly. In contrast, the dialogue and historical references used to give depth to *Beacon Hill* were heavy-handed. In the final analysis, the costumes and set were the best part of the show. It is best simply to forget *Beacon Hill.*

CLASSIC DIALOGUE

HACKER (*to a new hired hand*): "I control every minute of the Lassiters' lives, and they are no more aware of my manipulation than they are of God's."

BEN LASSITER: "The only people worth a damn are the takers. . . . The givers just keep the religions and charity rolling."

HACKER (*about his employers*): "The rich are children."

BEN LASSITER: "I was a country boy myself. It makes me immune to the blarney of country louts."

SOME KIND WORDS FROM ...

Arthur Unger of the *Christian Science Monitor*:
"A fiasco on every level."

Richard Schickel in *Time* magazine:
". . . [*Upstairs, Downstairs*'] vulgar American cousin, . . . commercial television once again refusing to trust the intelligence of its audience. . . ."

Harry F. Waters of *Newsweek*:
"An estimated 20 million Americans regularly watch TV soap operas. The question is: how many of them stay up until 10 P.M. on Tuesdays?"

The *New York Times*:
"Well, there were no plastic flowers. . . ."

Stephen Elliott (*seated*) and George Rose portrayed Lassiter and Hacker, each a key character in the *Beacon Hill* saga.

(*above*) Nancy Marchand and Stephen Elliott, Mr. and Mrs. Benjamin Lassiter of Beacon Hill, a posh section of Boston in the 1920s. "They had no concept of what the show was supposed to be," complained Ms. Marchand, who uniformly rewrote all of her lines to conform with the character she was attempting to develop.

(*right*) George Rose (*center*), who played Arthur Hacker, head butler in the Lassiter household, was the only British member of the cast. Did he think *Beacon Hill* was "quality" television? "No, I don't think quality TV can sell cupcakes. I grew up under a much freer system in England where quality television doesn't have to sell cupcakes and the like. In this country, there is no other reason for television to exist," remarked the distinguished actor, pictured here with Beatrice Straight and Paul Rudd.

Beatrice Straight, as Emmeline Hacker, comforts Rosamond Lassiter, played by Kitty Winn. The reviews *were* pretty awful.

Beacon Hill's only ray of hope, a character called Fawn Lassiter played by Kathryn Walker. She was the Bohemian of the family, a free spirit bent on modeling herself on Isadora Duncan.

FROM THE HORSE'S . . . (Beryl Vertue)

Q: Why did *Beacon Hill* bomb?

A: I don't feel it failed. What I had set out to do and what I achieved was to get together some of the best actors in New York and the best production team and do a really good drama series and also to do something different on American television for a change.

Q: Then why do you think the series was canceled?

A: To stay on American TV, you've got to be number one in the ratings, and we weren't. In the end, it got all out of proportion—I felt I was supposed to produce something miraculous . . . which I never promised to do.

Q: But the ratings kept plummeting . . .

A: I don't know who those people with the [Nielsen] machines are. Everywhere I went people told me how much they liked the show.

THE BUSINESS BEHIND THE BOX

Attempting to sort through the charges and countercharges leveled against CBS's embattled *Beacon Hill* is like trying to unravel a tangled ball of yarn. The blame rests, according to people connected with the 1975 effort, on various and sundry factors: over-promotion, bad writing, a lousy time slot, hokey dialogue, you name it.

Hoping to gain a lap or two on the competition, CBS premiered *Beacon Hill* as a two-hour "special" on August 25, two weeks or so before the fall season officially kicked off. Executives explained that the two-week jump on the other new shows would enable viewers to become familiar with the many *Beacon Hill* characters, some twenty in all. "The public will have to *work* when watching this show," remarked CBS vice-president Alan Wagner. "It's either going to be a tremendous success or fall flat on its face."

Well, as most TV-addict earthlings know, the show was *not* a tremendous success. It wasn't even a small success. It was, indeed, a "fall-flat-on-its-face" disaster. How could this admitted Americanized *Upstairs, Downstairs* fail when its British cousin was considered a milestone of the medium?

Let's start from *before* the beginning. Britisher Beryl Vertue started out as a secretary to two BBC comedy writers, Alan Simpson and Ray Galton. At her bosses' insistence, she moved up to become a literary agent, managing in the process to sell several properties, including *Steptoe and Son* and *Til Death Us Do Part* to British television. (A few years later she resold them to America, via Norman Lear, and they became *Sanford and Son* and *All in the Family.*) Another of Vertue's clients, Jean Marsh, had an idea for a show she called *Upstairs, Downstairs.*

Beryl managed to peddle that one too, with well-known results, before accepting an executive producership with the Robert Stigwood Organization where she was quickly assigned to the movie version of the rock opera *Tommy.*

Beryl's dream, however, was to fashion an American adaptation of *Upstairs, Downstairs* that would be just as successful. She sold the idea to CBS who was eager to be the first to offer "quality programing" (an oft-quoted and magniloquent misnomer of the day) to the hungry Yankee masses. Money would be no object. Only the best period costumes, antiques and vintage autos would be used. Only·the finest actors, to be gleaned from the New York stage, would be cast. Even Oscar-winning Marvin Hamlisch was signed to pen the score. The writing and direction would be supervised by two stalwart veterans of TV's "Golden Age," Sidney Carroll and Fielder Cook. This was going to be a class operation, there were no two ways about it.

A two-hour pilot, taped at Studio 41 in the CBS Broadcast Center in New York, cost more than $900,000 to produce. The company had exactly six days in which to rehearse and film 120 minutes of tricky 1920s dialogue to have it ready in time for an August 25 air date.

At nine o'clock that infamous summer eve, *Beacon Hill* made its auspicious debut, heralded by the CBS ballyhoo that called it "a dramatic series on a grand scale," a "gripping, powerful and compelling drama." The ratings were fantastic, but the critical opinion was decidedly mixed. The majority of reviews neither panned nor puffed, merely acknowledging that *Beacon Hill* was prime-time soap. Few could help but lavish praise on the evident authenticity.

Internal rumblings, however, were rampant among cast and crew. Nancy Marchand, the distinguished actress who played one of the leads and who now costars on *Lou Grant,* remembers: "As soon as the actors saw the first script, we were suicidal. Where was all that 'quality' they were talking about?"

Paul Rudd, who played chauffeur Brian Mallory, was equally unimpressed by the literary quality of the material. "The first line they had me saying was 'Top o' the mornin' to you.' No Irishman, outside of Bing Crosby in some movie, ever said that," Rudd reveals. "It got so bad that the producer had to tell us not to laugh at the scripts when the writers were present."

Sidney Carroll, premiere scriptwriter: "I wrote the pilot. My responsibility ended there. I was subsequently hired to come up with the first thirteen plots to follow the pilot. I did that, but when I saw what they were doing to my stories, I raised loud objections. I got nowhere and I quit."

"I gave them what I thought were thirteen good plot lines," continues Carroll, a noted screenwriter with a long list of admirable credits including the *Hallmark Hall of Fame.* "I assumed that they would confer with me about changes in those lines. I quit when I discovered that they were altering my stories, my plots, my characters—cheapening them, dirtying them up—without even the courtesy of a consultation call. I not only resigned, I actually tried to get my name off the screen, but they told me it was too late."

The first episode had not even aired and already the show had no story editor to oversee the continuity and quality of the scripts. The slide to oblivion had begun. "After the third show—a dog—I got a call from Fielder Cook, who had directed the pilot," says Carroll. "We agreed that something had to be done to save our brainchild. He suggested that we drop everything on our own agenda and offer to go back and do a couple of episodes to get back on the track. We made the offer. Do you know what the answer was? 'No thanks. We are perfectly satisfied with the show as it stands. We like it.'

"CBS actually *liked* it," Carroll recalls with a hint of incredulity. "This brass and the management thought it was a good show. The public kept telling them otherwise by deserting in droves."

As the situation and ratings worsened, last ditch efforts were made to save the show. John Hawkesworth, the producer of the original *Upstairs, Downstairs,* was called forth to help with the thirteenth episode. Surely if anyone could save the day, Hawkesworth could. He totally rewrote the script, stressing character, the quality that had distinguished *Upstairs, Downstairs.* According to many, it was by far the best episode.

However, Alan Wagner, the CBS man in charge said, "I found it a little bit talky. It was well written and beautifully performed and directed, but only a small part of it was germane. There would have been no impact on American audiences."

So, instead, on November 4, 1975, the eleventh episode became the final one; *Beacon Hill* was laid to rest in full view of 20 million people. At the time of its demise, the show was appealing mainly to older women, had substandard male appeal and absolutely no youth following to speak of. It had the third-lowest rating in television.

The implication was, of course, that the American public just was not ready to accept high-quality, top caliber television.

Nonsense. *Beacon Hill* blew it all by itself. Its failure was not the failure of the American audiences at all; it was the failure of American network television—and the caliber of its executives. In the final analysis, the professional skills and judgment, the coordination, the creativity, the sensitivity, the objectivity—the *quality*—was simply not present.

American audiences are still waiting for quality television. We resent second-rate programing when it is wrapped in cheap tinsel and labeled "quality."

THE BIG PARTY

THE GUILTY PARTIES

Creator:	Goodman Ace
Producer:	Perry Lafferty
Director:	Norman Jewison
Dialogue Director:	Abe Burrows
Writers:	Goodman Ace, George Foster, Selma Diamond, Jay Burton
Orchestra:	Gordon Jenkins

A Goodman Ace Production in association with Revlon, Inc., for CBS-TV.
Starring various "hosts" (Greer Garson, Douglas Fairbanks, Jr., Rock Hudson) and Barbara Britton for Revlon.
Debuted Thursday, October 8, 1959, 9:30 P.M. E.D.T. on CBS-TV.

THE FORMAT

The idea was tried, but not so true. Back in the late 1930s, NBC attempted a radio show titled *The Circle*. The premise was rotating emcees who would operate in a very informal and relaxed atmosphere for the purpose of conversation. Ronald Colman, Cary Grant, Carole Lombard, Groucho Marx, and Basil Rathbone did the so-called honors for sponsor Kellogg's, but the show neither snapped, crackled, nor popped, and faded into oblivion after a few painful months.

Never known to let sleeping dogs lie, TV resurrected the radio idea ten years later, calling it *Penthouse Party*. The ABC show featured Betty Furness as hostess to a conglomeration of celebrities whom she invites into the living room of her New York penthouse. This one died fast, too. CBS obviously decided that ABC did it wrong on TV and that NBC fouled it up on radio, so they put together a fifteen-minute show (this one would be only half-bad) starring Ilka Chase—with

Durwood Kirby—called *Glamour-Go-Round* (Durwood provided the glamour). This one was set in Miss Chase's drawing room where the doorbell would chime and in would come, say, Abe Burrows. They would chat about the weather, President Truman, and Abe's next Broadway show. This show, like its predecessors, limped through six long months before keeling over.

A decade later, writer Goodman Ace, hired away from Perry Como to formulate Revlon's new variety show for CBS, "created" *The Big Party:* an "informal, relaxed" show featuring a "conglomeration of celebrities" in a "glamour" setting. The *TV Guide* description of the first show pretty much characterizes the entire series of six "big parties": "Rock Hudson comes to New York City, moves into a hotel and decides to throw a party. He asks his pal Tallulah Bankhead to get on the phone and invite some friends. Tallulah calls Sammy Davis, Jr., Matt Dennis, Lisa Kirk, Carlos Montoya, Mort Sahl, and Esther Williams. *The Big Party* is ready to start."

Rock wasn't much help as the host, lending neither authority nor personality to his chore. He fell flat when he attempted to sing a medley of songs with Esther Williams, who looked lost without her bathing suit. Frankly, the guests should have graciously declined Tallulah's invitation.

The frequent on-stage commercials for Revlon products didn't help much, nor did the flustered Barbara Britton, spokeswoman for the cosmetics firm, who couldn't quite master the segues from show to commercial and back again. One reviewer called her "a party-pooper of the first magnitude." She wasn't the only one "pooped" by this party.

Subsequent segments, featuring Greer Garson and Douglas Fairbanks, Jr. as hosts of the imaginary parties, were no more effective. In fact, the proceedings went progressively downhill. Any program that paired José Greco and Chuck "Rifleman" Connors on one outing needed a lot of help.

After the second "party," *Daily Variety* commented, "If anything can bring quiz shows back to CBS, *The Big Party* may do it."

MEMORABLE MOMENTS

- Martha Raye singing "Mr. Paganini."
- Greer Garson doing impressions of famous people.
- Sal Mineo warbling "Mack the Knife."
- A commercial featuring Gloria Swanson shaving Ramon Novarro's face with a Schick.
- Rock Hudson and Esther Williams dueting "How About You?"

SOME KIND WORDS FROM ...

Dwight Whitney of *TV Guide:*
***"The Big Party* is a big bore!"**

Daily Variety:
**"The whole is not necessarily equal
to the sum of its parts.... Fell flatter
than a pancake ... a drag ...
awkward, it flopped. ..."**

Arthur Shulman and Roger Youman
in *How Sweet It Was:*
"Absurd."

Rock Hudson played host to Sammy
Davis, Jr., who sang "Let's Get Away From
It All," and Tallulah Bankhead, who
showed us how to use the telephone on the
October 8 *Big Party.* Other guests included
Mort Sahl, Carlos Montoya, and Esther
Williams.

Hostess Greer Garson, about to portray Eleanor Roosevelt in the film *Sunrise At Campobello,* invited Martha Raye and the comedy team of Mike Nichols and Elaine May to the October 22 bash. John Bubbles and Peter Lind Hayes were on hand, too.

Douglas Fairbanks, Jr. threw the December 3 soiree, inviting the likes of Danny Thomas and Bobby Darin. Nichols and May returned for an encore.

FROM THE HORSE'S ... (*Goodman Ace*)

Q: What was the show's original concept?

A: I had conceived the show as a kind of show business party—a bunch of actors sitting around discussing politics, show business, anything. Then someone would go to the piano and do a song or two.

Q: What happened between the idea and its execution?

A: Charles Revson and I had a couple of run-ins before the first show. He'd talk about the master of ceremonies, and I'd say, "But there *is* no emcee." Then he'd mention the runway the guest stars would come out on, and I'd say, "But there *is* no runway." I finally told him, "I think they've sold you the wrong show."

Q: How did you resolve this obvious difference of opinion?

A: After the first show, the thing became a mess. Revson thought singing and dancing were the only kind of entertainment there is. They cut out the dialogue almost completely. There were actually meetings in which show business was explained to me. I don't know what they thought—that they had picked me off the streets, maybe. At the end, I told them, "I did the best *you* could."

THE BUSINESS BEHIND THE BOX

Charles Revson, patriarch of the cosmetics giant, Revlon, made great corporate strides as sponsor of *The $64,000 Question*, CBS's premiere big-money game show of the 1950s. Prior to its association with the popular quiz show, Revlon was lagging well behind its competitor, Hazel Bishop, in sales, but within a matter of months after *Question's* debut, sales of "Living Lipstick," Revlon's key product (promoted on the air by adorable Wendy Barrie) skyrocketed. The 47 million *Question* viewers—half of them women—responded en masse to the sponsor's pitches. Revlon quickly grabbed the Number One spot from Hazel Bishop.

When the "high stakes" game shows were driven off the air in the fall of 1958 because of substantiated and rumored deception, Revlon was caught without a major TV show to sponsor. At the same time, CBS decided to cut back its weekly anthology *Playhouse 90* to every-other-week status after three seasons of the week-in-week-out grind. The network made a deal with Revlon's ad agency to sponsor a "unique variety show" to alternate with *Playhouse 90*. Revlon went directly to Goodman Ace, then dean of comedy writers, asking him to create and ultimately write their new "unique variety show."

Ace, who had spent thirty years writing radio and TV scripts, could hardly ignore Revlon's offer. While his exact salary was never disclosed, it was much more than he was getting as Perry Como's head writer, a tidy $11,500 a week, the most money paid to a TV comedy writer up to that time (Jess Oppenheimer, at the height of *I Love Lucy's* popularity in 1955, was getting $2,500 a week for his writing *and* producing chores).

Vaguely resembling radio's *Big Show*, the format would be, according to Ace, "a high-class variety show with Shubert Alley talk. The guests will sit around and gab, and then maybe they'll get up and sing or dance, and then sit down and talk some more. This will be funny talk, mind you. The insults will fly. I hope we manage some smart observations on our times."

Prior to the show's October debut, Ace met routinely with his "boss," Revson. The makeup mogul told of *his* plans for the first program. Goody interrupted. As creator, he reminded Revson, he had artistic control over the first program, though not the latter ones. Revson, who fancied himself something of a show business expert, was downright annoyed, but his hands were contractually tied.

The first show of the series, titled *The Big Party By Revlon*, aired Thursday, October 8, 1959, with Rock Hudson as host of the so-called party. Hudson's appearance was for the sole purpose of plugging his new film with Doris Day, *Pillow Talk*. The show, though ambitious as hell, just did not come off. The true essence of any party is impossible to convey via cameras. And because it was totally written, any spontaneity that could have occurred was automatically squelched.

While the ratings were uniformly low, particularly outside urban markets, some reviews were not all that bad; some were downright exuberant in their praise of the program. John Lardner lauded Ace's brainchild in the *New Yorker*, and Bill Paley, president of CBS, thought it was "the best television show ever." Still, *Party* pooped out after six painful outings. And since Goodman Ace and Charles Revson did not exactly see eye-to-eye about the concept, they parted company amicably, tearing up the contract for fourteen more "unique" parties.

Most critics agreed that the show would have fared better as a straight variety program, perhaps even retaining the party "idea" but not taking it so seriously while trying to fool the viewing public into thinking it was a *real* party. Blame all that wasted effort to make the proceedings seem like the height of chichi sophistication, the phony chit-chat, the belabored introductions, the strained and awkward atmosphere between "acts."

Six months after wounds healed, Ace wrote his pen pal Groucho Marx: "I have been vegetating, as I realized that all too soon I've become a senior hack television writer, even to the point of permitting myself to be cajoled into doing the Como show again this coming season. I had made such splendid plans to stay out of TV this year, when Jane [Ace's wife] took over and told me it was about time I gave up this preposterous idea of making $25,000 a week doing that big show for Revlon. To quote her correctly: 'Do you have to take those jobs for $25,000 a week? Can't you get a job like everybody else for five or six thousand a week?'"

THE DAKOTAS

THE GUILTY PARTIES

Creator:	Robert E. Thompson
Supervising Producer:	Jules Schermer
Producer:	Anthony Spinner
Director:	Stuart Heisler, et al.
Writers:	Cy Chermak,
	Richard Landau, et al.
Cameraman:	Bert Glennon
Film Editor:	Robert Wolfe

A Warner Brothers Television production for ABC-TV.
Starring Larry Ward as Marshal Frank Ragan, Jack Elam as J. D. Smith, Chad Everett as Del Stark, and Michael Greene as Vance Porter.
Debuted Monday, January 7, 1963, 7:30 P.M. E.S.T. on ABC-TV.

THE FORMAT

It was nothing more than routine horse opera, a throwback to the 1950s-era westerns with run-of-the-mill writing, uninspired direction, and pedestrian acting— falling into the if-you've-seen-one-you've-seen-'em-all category. No different from *Tate, Shotgun Slade, Tombstone Territory,* etc.

The Dakotas refers, of course, to the U.S. territory of the 1880s, and a wild, woolly and crime-ridden region of western America it was, at least according to this show's premise. Marshal Frank Ragan (Larry Ward) is responsible for maintaining law and order. He has the help of three deputies: J. D. Smith (Jack Elam), Del Stark (Chad Everett), and Vance Porter (Michael Greene). This trio of aides is more of a burden to the marshal than a help. Reformed gunfighter Smith, for instance, is forever shooting first and reasoning later. He just can't keep his finger off the trigger, and the marshal can't stop telling him to tone down his gunside manner. Unfortunately, the marshal doesn't fire the underling, which of course he should. "I need his gun," says the marshal, "and as long as I do, he'll keep the badge on."

All nineteen *Dakotas* episodes were basically the same show with different titles—"Mutiny at Fort Mercy," "Trouble at French Creek," "Thunder in Pleasant Valley," "Feud at Snake River." (Luckily the show got a quick cancellation—they might have run out of catchy locales!)

We don't think that *The Dakotas* was really any worse than some of its western cousins, but it *did* deserve singling out as an example of "too much already."

CLASSIC DIALOGUE:

FATHER (*to his mischievous son*):   "Go to your horse!"

JUDGE HARVEY (*to Marshal Ragan*):   "Don't interrupt me, Marshal. I'm in the middle of a sentence."

INDIAN (*about to be lynched*):   "For us there is no justice. There is only pride."

FATHER (*to his erring offspring*):   "It ain't right, son. A boy and his pa has just got to talk."

MARSHAL RAGAN (*to one unjustly accused*):   "You're not the only one on trial. We're all on trial here."

Granite-jawed Larry Ward rated top billing on ABC's *Dakotas.* He played Frank Ragan, marshal of the Dakota Territory of the 1880s. Ward put behind him a career as a budding playwright (*Rhom, Masterpiece*) to take on the bad guys on the Warner backlot.

After playing the "heavy" on some 100 TV shows, Jack Elam was cast as a good guy—a deputy sheriff, no less—on Warner Brothers' *Dakotas* series. "I got such a good deal from them that I'll bet they drop me from the show in a year—they can't afford it!" said Elam, claiming, "My face is all I've got." Columnist Vernon Scott once wrote: "He makes Boris Karloff look like Tab Hunter."

Ray Crampton, better known as Chad Everett, *Medical Center*'s Dr. Joe Gannon, came to Hollywood from Dearborn, Michigan, lucked out as a contract player at Warner Brothers—one of fifty hired during the early 1960s—and found himself acting in such TV shows as *Hawaiian Eye*, *SurfSide 6*, *77 Sunset Strip*, *Maverick*, etc. Then *The Dakotas* rode the video plains, and Everett began his rise to stardom.

A scene from the premiere episode of *The Dakotas,* "Return to Dryrock," features series regulars Larry Ward (*in background*) and Chad Everett, with guest star Natalie Trundy as "Betty Lou." The show never achieved the high ratings its predecessor, *Cheyenne,* did, and was dropped after nineteen episodes.

THE BUSINESS BEHIND THE BOX

During the 1958 TV season, there were forty westerns riding the video range, most of them on the networks; a few in syndication. Oaters, as they are called in the industry, were in their heyday (sorry) in the late 1950s. By the end of September 1959, there were thirty-two shoot-'em-ups on the air, some nine of them landing in Nielsen's Top Twenty list for the year, including such staples as *Gunsmoke*, *Wagon Train*, *Rifleman*, *Cheyenne*, and *Wanted—Dead or Alive*.

Then the bottom of the buckboard began falling out, and by 1962 there were only four westerns in the Top Twenty, and that number dwindled to two the following year (*Gunsmoke* and *Bonanza*). It was the beginning of the end of an era.

The Dakotas rode into view in 1963 over the aged bones of ABC's *Cheyenne* series. Clint Walker had gotten fed up playing the frontier scout Bodie after seven and a half years in the Warner Brothers western, its first successful TV series, and quit. The same studio slapped together *The Dakotas*, and ABC agreed to use it as *Cheyenne*'s replacement when the latter finished up its fall 1962 run of thirteen episodes.

The story of a frontier marshal and his three hard-riding, hard-shooting deputies operating in the Dakota territory of the 1880s starred a quartet of actors not terribly well known to TV audiences. Only one, Jack Elam, had achieved any notoriety prior to *The Dakotas*—and this mostly for his many roles as a villain. Elam, a one-time CPA for the film industry, played Deputy J. D. Smith, a reformed gunfighter. "I'm ashamed to be seen wearing a badge in *The Dakotas*," he once confided to a journalist, "so I kind of hide it under my vest. And every time I have to bad-mouth the heavies, the words stick in my throat."

Another deputy was portrayed by a youthful Chad Everett, more than six years before he won the role of Dr. Joe Gannon on CBS's *Medical Center* series. Everett, a Warner's contract player, was not content with his part in the western: "It wasn't suited to me. There were too many stars and they had me holding horses for about eleven out of nineteen segments. I don't hold horses very well."

The series premiered in the wake of *Cheyenne*'s cancellation on Monday, January 7, 1963, and became ABC's lead-in show to *Rifleman*, *Stoney Burke*, and *Ben Casey*. Its strongest competition came in the form of a pair of Goodson-Todman game shows, *I've Got a Secret* and *To Tell the Truth*, both of which regularly figured in Nielsen's Top Twenty list. *The Dakotas* never had a chance.

"I thought if I could get a TV series," *Dakota*'s Chad Everett once said, "I'd be at the top of the ladder. Well, I got the series, but I found it was the bottom of the ladder."

GET CHRISTIE LOVE!

THE GUILTY PARTIES

Creators:	Peter Nelson, George Kirgo
	(based on a novel by Dorothy Uhnak)
Executive Producer:	David Wolper
Producers:	Paul Mason, Glen A. Larson, Ron Satlof
Associate Producer:	Mervin Dayan
Directors:	Mark Warren, Gene Nelson, et al.
Writers:	Calvin Clements, Albert E. Lewin,
	Robert Earll, David P. Lewis,
	Brad Radnitz, et al.
Cameraman:	Stanley Lazan
Film Editor:	Robert Shugrue
Art Director:	Seymour Klate
Music by:	Lucci De Jesus
Casting:	Milt Hammerman

A Wolper Production in association with Universal Television for ABC-TV.
Starring Teresa Graves as Christie Love, Charles Cioffi as Lieutenant Matt Reardon, Jack Kelly as Captain Arthur P. Ryan, Andy Romano as Detective Joe Caruso, Dennis Rucker as Detective Steve Belmont, Scott Peters as Detective Valencia, and Michael Pataki as Sergeant Pete Gallagher.
Debuted Wednesday, September 11, 1974, 10 P.M. E.D.T. on ABC-TV.

THE FORMAT

"Beauty, brains and a badge!" promised ABC's embarrassing ads for *Get Christie Love!*, a bit of cop tripe the network offered its 1974 audience. The story of a brassy, sassy undercover detective with the Special Investigations Division of the Los Angeles Police Department. A lady who not only gets her man, but who also gets to sass him as she slips on the handcuffs. "You're under arrest, sugar," Christie repeats in every raunchy episode.

Once a "street kid," Christie (Teresa Graves) gets tired of being a "down thing" and decides quite positively to become a policewoman. She succeeds quickly, and is promoted to undercover work (and a changing wardrobe). Her tough no-nonsense police boss, Lieutenant Matt Reardon (Charles Cioffi) is a model of every tough, no-nonsense boss who has appeared on a TV cop show.

If Christie is up against four or five ex-football player types turned bad boys—no problem: she gives them a few trusty arm thrusts, a few swift kicks to the head and whammo!—they are arrested and convicted just like that! That bitch is deadly, no two ways about it.

The *Get Christie Love!* plots—all twenty-two of them—were typical TV fare. In other words, they were lousy. Christie out to bust up a narcotics ring, Christie up against an older and prejudiced police captain, Christie infiltrating a stolen goods operation, etc. One episode even reunited star Teresa Graves with her former *Laugh-In* cohort: Arte Johnson, Henry Gibson, Jo Anne Worley, Judy Carne, Johnny Brown, and Gary Owens, in an effort to beef up sagging ratings. In another segment, tennis greats Bobby Riggs and Rosemary Casals were featured. Nothing helped.

"How great it will be for young black women watching the show," said *Christie* producer Paul Mason, "to see one of their sisters on the right side of the law."

Get *Christie Love!* wasn't on the right side of anything. It was a crime in itself.

MEMORABLE MOMENTS

- Posing as an aspiring singer, Christie tries to snare a sinister record company owner suspected of murdering his most popular artist.

- Christie becomes a student aviatrix in an effort to learn whether the owner of the flying school is in cahoots with an escaped thief.

- Christie pops up as a stewardess after an inventive smuggler forces Captain Ryan to accompany him on a flight to London.

CLASSIC DIALOGUE

CHRISTIE: "Your only crime so far is MMT!" [Making Me Tired].

MOTORCYCLE GANG LEADER: "Why don't you go back to L.A.?"
CHRISTIE: "And give up all this fresh country air?
CHRISTIE: You're under arrest, sugar."

SOME KIND WORDS FROM . . .

Cleveland Amory of *TV Guide*:
"Christie isn't very believable, but compared to the show around her, she's the oracle of Delphi . . ."

Daily Variety:
". . . drenched with inadequate scripts, listless direction, and a preposterous concept."

Ms. magazine:
". . . resembles black exploitation movies starring karate-chopping women."

TV's tamed-down answer to the popular Black exploitation films of the 1970s was *Get Christie Love!* starring ex-*Laugh-In* regular Teresa Graves. Here she poses with a couple of pigeons, presumably part of the show's following.

"Don't ever underestimate Christie Love. She's all cop!" is what the ABC publicity department churned out in the way of hype when the series premiered in 1974. Teresa Graves played the jive-talkin', karate-choppin' law enforcer in this run-of-the-mill "copper."

Christie in one of her high-fashion costumes. Graves: "I'm an actress doing a part, but I am very pleased that I am playing the lead in a dramatic series."

YOU'RE UNDER ARREST, SUGAR

Ad nauseam is the Latin phrase for "to a sickening degree." "You're under arrest, sugar" fits the bill.

THE BUSINESS BEHIND THE BOX

It had to happen. Right on the heels of those early 1970s super-popular Black exploitation films—*Shaft, Superfly, Cotton Comes to Harlem*—a TV series, a distaff version of the jive flicks, called *Get Christie Love!*

Spunky, funky Christie Love saw the light of day in a novel by Dorothy Uhnak which producer David (*Roots*) Wolper bought and brought to TV via a ninety-minute ABC Movie-of-the-Week, telecast January 22, 1974. Starring pert and perky Teresa Graves, late of *Laugh-In,* as Christie, with Harry Guardino as her boss, the TV movie racked up some impressive ratings and a goodly amount of positive fan mail. ABC, battling to get a foothold in the ratings war, decided that the *Christie* concept had some potential as a weekly series and promptly scheduled it for the upcoming 1974–75 fall season. Teresa would retain her role as the cool, sexy, smart-mouth undercover cop, and Charles Cioffi was signed to take over the Guardino role. It sounded good on paper.

"I like the character," said Teresa Graves, onetime singer with the Doodletown Pipers and the Young Americans. "Christie's bright, young and kicky. She knows her business but she's a lady. She's fun. It's not hard for me to relate to her. She's kind of me, in a way. She does everything professionally. I could read the script and see myself. I had no apprehension about doing the part or being her. She's not a superwoman. She's tough, but she's still a woman. She cries when she's hurt."

Ms. Graves, in fact, was not producer Wolper's first choice for the role. Cicely Tyson was signed and ready to shoot the TV movie in November 1973 when, at the last minute, she suffered a severe foot injury which necessitated her withdrawal from the project. The show was all but abandoned until someone in the Wolper office remembered Graves.

But who could ever forget Teresa Graves? Her sleek bronze body was bared weekly for 40 million viewers of *Laugh-In* back in the late 1960s, after staff makeup artists painted on her body such witticisms as "Mercy Mercy," "Flower Power," "Ring My Chimes," and "Here Come De Judge." After the Rowan and Martin show, Graves did a pilot with Flip Wilson that didn't sell, toured Vietnam with Bob Hope, and filmed a couple of Blacksploitation movies with Fred Williamson that led directly to her being signed for *Get Christie Love!*

Her contract with the producers was unique. Because of her devotion to the Jehovah Witnesses faith, Teresa was allowed two days off each year to attend the annual J. W. rally at Dodger Stadium in Los Angeles. Also, she was to be released from shooting two days per week at 5 P.M. (most shows rehearse and film until 8 or 9 P.M.) to give her ample time to pursue her Bible studies and read *Awake,* the Witness magazine. It was further stipulated that Christie never kill anyone on the show, never tell a direct lie, and that no profanity was to be uttered. What's a cop show without killing, lying, and swearing?

"In the pilot, Christie was fending off six guys with karate in a situation that was totally unbelievable," stated producer Paul Mason during the filming of the *Get Christie Love!* series. "In the show we'll have plenty of action, but when she uses her karate, which will not be very often, it will be in a realistic situation.

"What I am not taking out is the irrepressible personality of Christie. She loves to have a good time and she has a great sense of humor. We are retaining the phrase, 'You're under arrest, sugar' and we'll use it a lot."

Mason's quest for realism was short-lived. The ABC network began to dictate story concepts, and by the time the series premiered on Wednesday, September 11, 1974, it was nothing more than a routine cop show. The only difference was that it starred a black woman. That night the three networks began a heads-on battle for the time slot—each web debuted a new one-hour drama series. NBC put up *Petrocelli,* a series about a lawyer in the Southwest starring Barry Newman, and CBS offered *Manhunter,* a throwaway series about a bountyhunter starring Ken Howard. The only show of the three that made any noise was the NBC outing, eventually lasting two seasons.

Get Christie Love! a low budget show by all of TV's standards that depended totally on the drawing power of Teresa Graves, sank in the Nielsen ratings pool. The network's attempt at rescheduling it in April 1975—stupidly putting it against NBC's *Policewoman*—did nothing to help the matter. *Christie* was dead by Christmas; even Santa couldn't spread cheer.

The only thing left was for someone to deliver a yuletide message to Teresa Graves: "You're canceled, sugar!"

GILLIGAN'S ISLAND

THE GUILTY PARTIES

Creator:	Sherwood Schwartz
Producers:	Sherwood Schwartz, Jack Arnold
Directors:	John Rich, Jack Arnold, Gary Nelson
Writers:	Sherwood Schwartz, Al Schwartz,
	Elroy Schwartz, Budd Grossman,
	Joanna Lee, Austin Kalish,
	Lawrence J. Cohen, Fred Freeman
Cameraman:	Richard Rawlings
Film Editor:	Larry Heath
Art Director:	Craig Smith
Music by:	Frank Comstock, Johnny Williams,
	Herschel Burke Gilbert

A Gladasya Production for United Artists Television in association with CBS-TV.

Starring Bob Denver as Gilligan, Alan Hale, Jr. as the Skipper, Jim Backus as Thurston Howell III, Natalie Schafer as Mrs. Lovey Howell, Tina Louise as Ginger Grant, Russell Johnson as the Professor, and Dawn Wells as Mary Ann Summers.

Debuted Saturday, September 26, 1964, 8:30 P.M. E.D.T. on CBS-TV.

THE FORMAT

"Now sit right back and you'll hear a tale. . . ." begins the unfortunately unforgettable *Gilligan's Island* theme song which goes on, *ad nauseum,* to inform us musically that (1) the *S.S. Minnow* is a "tiny ship," (2) the mate is "mighty," (3) the skipper "brave and sure," (4) there are five passengers aboard, (5) the cruise was supposed to take only three hours, (6) out at sea a storm materializes, (7) the ship is grounded on an "uncharted desert isle," and (8) aside from (first and only mate) Gilligan and the Skipper, there are a millionaire couple, a movie star, a professor, and a Mary Ann. Simple enough. Seemingly harmless.

What the opening film and song do not explain is how, just a few miles off the coast of Hawaii, a storm so violent could maroon this septet of goons on an island so remote that no one can find them. It doesn't explain to us why most of these characters are on the ill-fated boat in the first place.

Take the millionaire and his wife—Mr. and Mrs. Thurston Howell III (Jim Backus and Natalie Schafer), for instance. He is the bombastic but benevolent chairman of the board of Howell Industries, an enormously wealthy corporation, and his blue-blooded spouse is a snooty but lovable Grosse Pointe bitch. They are so rich that they just happen to bring along a suitcase full of money.

And the movie star, Ginger Grant (Tina Louise)—she's supposed to be a glamorous Hollywood starlet, a Marilyn Monroe type. It is revealed that she was entertaining at a USO show and got bored (with 6,000 horny Marines?) so hopped aboard the *Minnow* . . . in a sequined gown.

Then there's the Professor (Russell Johnson), who's thirty-five, handsome, and from Cleveland. His specialty is—get this—dull metals. He is at work on a book *Rust: The Real Red Menace,* but went along on the sightseeing cruise to study local flora and fauna. (Just what type of flora and fauna one can study aboard a ship is beyond us.) At any rate, he's very helpful: He can fashion cups from coconuts, "silverware" out of bamboo, and lipstick for Ginger made of raspberries. Using bicycle wheels and a pair of pedals (don't ask us who brought these along on the boat), he manages to manufacture all manner of things—everything, of course, but a seaworthy raft to float to shore!

Mary Ann Summers (Dawn Wells), a nineteen-year-old farm girl who hails from Plainview, Kansas, is the archetypal all-American youth, and probably the only truly logical *Minnow* passenger. She won her passage, her first trip away from home, through a contest sponsored by a romance magazine. Exuding Pollyanna sweetness in sickening proportions, Mary Ann actually enjoys being stranded on the island. So much for life in Plainview.

The Laurel and Hardy of the group (also the stars of the show) are Gilligan (Bob Denver) and the Skipper (Alan Hale, Jr.). The rotund, jovial but short-tempered skipper of the *Minnow* is a physical brute of a man whom according to his creator, Sherwood Schwartz, "believes the proper solution to everything is to run roughshod, and as skipper gives orders because that's all he knows."

The man he hired as mate—a cartoon character come to life—Gilligan has one ambition in life: to do something right, just once. Born under the sign Inept, he has a penchant for screwing up every imaginable rescue plan. It was, after all, his fault that the *Minnow* was wrecked in the first place: He lost the anchor, smashed the compass, and broke the transmitter. Three strikes but not out.

For three tedious years, the seven castaways struggle to make ends meet on the tiny island where they have been stranded with the Professor's books, Mrs. Howell's jewelry collection, Ginger's entire Hollywood wardrobe, Thurston's hat rack of hats, everything—everything but a funny script.

MEMORABLE MOMENTS

▪ Gilligan and the skipper think they're seeing things: A surfer has just ridden onto the island.

▪ An ape sneaks into camp and makes off with Mrs. Howell's valuable diamond brooch.

▪ Trouble breaks out when a native king arrives to find a goddess . . . heavenly enough to be fed to a volcano.

▪ Howell turns detective to find out who's been sending unsigned love notes to his wife.

A scene from the premiere episode, "Two On a Raft." Based on this sample showing, *Gilligan's Island* amassed the worst collection of opening night notices since *The Beverly Hillbillies. Variety* claimed "the castaways could have walked the water to safety on the bones of some of these ancient gags."

Jim Backus played Thurston Howell III, a millionaire that Sherwood Schwartz modeled after Backus's own "Hubert Updyke" character. Here he is pictured with Natalie Schafer (*left*) who played his wife Lovey, and Zsa Zsa Gabor, who apparently discovered the remote island on the way to her next wedding.

Alan Hale, Jr. said he had absolutely no faith in the series before it was scheduled and guaranteed for twenty-six weeks. Bob Denver, likewise, had his reservations after four comfortable years as Maynard G. Krebs on the *Dobie Gillis* series: "Sherwood outlined thirty-six premises for me in ten minutes. After that I didn't ask any more questions. I figured if he could come up with that many ideas that fast, there wasn't any problem!"

Fourteen years after the *Minnow* sailed on CBS, Alan Hale, Jr. and Bob Denver returned to the small screen as the Skipper and Gilligan in *Rescue From Gilligan's Island*, a 1978 NBC special. The two-hour two-parter reunited all of the regulars, except Tina Louise. It seems Ms. Louise and the six other members of the original cast never got along.

The "seven stranded castaways" of *Gilligan's Island:* (*l. to r.*) Russell Johnson (the Professor), Alan Hale, Jr. (the Skipper), Bob Denver (Gilligan), Dawn Wells (Mary Ann Summers), Tina Louise (Ginger Grant), Jim Backus (Mr. Howell), and Natalie Schafer (Mrs. Howell). About *Gilligan's* critics, Ms. Schafer once remarked, "I don't know why they keep saying how bad we are—even if we are!"

"We have life-and-death stories," producer Sherwood Schwartz once insisted. "Will they survive? What if there is an earthquake?" What if Backus bogies the hole?

FROM THE HORSE'S ... (Jim Backus)

Q: How did you get involved in *Gilligan's Island?*
A: Sherwood Schwartz called me. . . . I'd worked with him on *I Married Joan* back in the 1950s . . . and said, "I've got a show I want you to do. But you can't see the script. If I showed it to you, you'd belt me."

Q: Was he correct?
A: I read it and he was right. The character had seven lines, but he promised me that if I did it, he'd build the part. I almost signed to do another pilot.

Q: Are you glad now that you signed to do *Gilligan's Island* and not another show?
A: The show is an annuity. The residuals keep rolling in. Of course, my reviews were something else. They were character assaults. I could have sued for defamation. They should have been written on the walls of a men's room.

THE BUSINESS BEHIND THE BOX

With a title partially plucked from the Los Angeles phone book, *Gilligan's Island* had its origins in another widely read literary work: *Robinson Crusoe.* Sherwood Schwartz, who once aspired to be a doctor but couldn't get into med school, unabashedly chose the Daniel Defoe classic as the model for his TV creation: "The book is in the top ten best-sellers of all time." With master's degrees in both zoology and psychology and an Emmy for writing excellence (the Red Skelton hour), Schwartz conceived his story of seven characters marooned on an uncharted, uninhabited Pacific Island in the spring of 1963: "I expected enormous resistance to the idea. After all, it dealt with people on a deserted island, and where do you go?"

But Schwartz was miraculously given the green light and a boodle of United Artists greenbacks to develop his concept within forty-eight hours of his agent's submission of the ten-page mimeographed outline/presentation. "What I hoped to portray were cliché characters," admits Schwartz. "If I had taken seven offbeat individuals that nobody was familiar with and put them in a jungle, the audience would not have understood what I was doing. Each had to represent a different segment of society so that anybody watching could identify with somebody."

The pilot, which cost $175,000 to film in a remote section of Kauai in Hawaii (the *I Love Lucy* pilot, in comparison, cost $16,000 thirteen years earlier), received varying degrees of enthusiasm from CBS, the network that partially financed the show. "Mike Dann, then vice president in charge of programing, told me it was the best idea for a situation comedy that he ever heard," Schwartz recalls. "Hunt

Stromberg, Jr., a West Coast vice president for CBS, was very very high on it, too. But Jim Aubrey, who was CBS president at the time, disliked the show immensely. He said, 'It's impossible—nobody can sustain such a series.' I told him it was not impossible, but it wasn't going to be easy. He tried to get me to change the whole concept."

Never-say-die Aubrey continued his assault on Schwartz's brainchild: "If you're in love with a deserted island, we wreck them there the first week. Then the second week they have a new adventure, they fix the boat and they're off someplace else," Aubrey suggested pointedly. The man, known in the business as "The Smiling Cobra," once phoned Jack Benny to tell him his program was being dropped. Instead of the usual amenities before the ax, Aubrey sneered: "You're through."

A completed version of the *Gilligan's* pilot was shipped to New York during the TV buying season. Schwartz, annoyed by the network tampering, appended a note to his film indicating that the finished product did not represent his original thinking. As expected, the series was summarily rejected by Aubrey.

But Schwartz refused to allow his *Robinson Crusoe* to sink. Though he had earlier fought futilely with United Artists' Dick Dorso to insert a lyrical musical theme in the opening—to explain the premise—Schwartz sat down at his baby grand and, with one finger, composed "The Ballad of Gilligan's Island," now a song classic among children twelve years of age and under.

He assembled all the pilot footage, hastily re-edited it, added his theme song, and air-mailed *his* version of *Gilligan's Island* back to New York for a second look. It was routinely audience-tested, and, according to Schwartz, "The results were phenomenal. But it was the final week of the selling season and they were locking up the fall schedule. At the eleventh hour, Aubrey softened and the show was on the schedule."

A few weeks later, Schwartz was called in for yet another network confab. "Who can identify with a Hollywood actress?" asked a CBS executive, referring to *Gilligan's* character Ginger Grant. "And who's going to understand a billionaire?" questioned another. "I was told that the professor was colorless—a high school science teacher—what kind of flair does that have?" Schwartz remembers. "The more they analyzed, the more faults they found."

Schwartz won the major battle—his seven characterizations remained intact, but CBS managed to triumph in another area. Three of the actors who appeared in the pilot were unacceptable, so the trio was discharged and replaced, requiring two extra days of shooting the new group for an updated pilot. Instead of Hawaii, the revamping was accomplished at Zuma Beach, a stretch of sand and surf between Malibu and Santa Barbara, California.

Even though Aubrey still didn't like the show, Gilligan's isle was erected, at a cost of $75,000, in the middle of a lake at CBS Studio Center, once the home of Republic Pictures. After the lake bottom was blacktopped and the water poured in, it leaked, so it had to be emptied, fixed and refilled. In the true Hollywood tradition, artificial palm trees and plastic flowers were "planted."

What finally reached the air on "opening night," Saturday, September 26, 1964, was a pastiche of three separate shows, including half of the pilot welded together by the CBS "committee." It was almost unanimously blasted by the critics. "I did not want this ersatz first show to air first," says Schwartz, today a millionaire from *Gilligan's Island* and his other creation, *The Brady Bunch.* "I wanted the pilot to air first. Unfortunately, I did not have complete creative control and I was overruled. So a show that had been projected as our second or third episode ["Two On a Raft"] was shown first. It was ridiculous. If you're telling a story about people who get shipwrecked, the only honest way is if the first show is about how they got wrecked. Instead, it was about how they were trying to get off the island. I think this affected the critics' reviews. Had it come later in the series, it would have been greeted in a different way."

Regardless of its cool critical reception, *Gilligan's Island* was a success with the viewers, never dropping out of the Top Forty during its first year. In fact, it placed #19 out of 117 shows with an average share of 38 percent of the audience for the entire season. Some weeks, it did better than *The Lucy Show,* and you can't do much better than that.

"Little kids seem to love *Gilligan's Island,*" says Bob Denver, star of the sitcom. "It doesn't take a mature intellect to laugh at a monkey running off with Gilligan's dinner or a guy getting hit on the head by a coconut." In syndication (there are ninety-eight episodes available) *Gilligan's Island* is unparalleled in popularity among children and teens.

Sherwood Schwartz, however, never agreed that the program was strictly a "kid's show": "It's basically a socially satirical show. We were poking fun at segments of society represented by the seven people on the island."

Kid's show or satire, *Gilligan's Island* remained on CBS three seasons and actually was scheduled for a fourth semester (it was #49 out of 113 shows). "*Gunsmoke* had been canceled after a run of about a dozen years," explains a member of the CBS research team. "With viewer reaction running unfavorably, William Paley himself demanded the reinstatement of the western on the fall schedule. But to accomplish this, we had to remove two marginal half-hours, *Run, Buddy, Run* and *Gilligan's Island.*"

Eleven years later in 1978, NBC—which would kill for a hit of any kind—went out and propositioned Sherwood Schwartz, then only tinkering part time in TV, and concluded a deal for him to produce, with the original cast, a two-part, two-hour "special," *Rescue From Gilligan's Island.* The script was as wretched as its ninety-eight predecessors, but the show got a 52 Nielsen share, ranking it among the Top Five shows of the week. Naturally, a few months later, a second "special" was telecast, *The Castaways on Gilligan's Island.*

We can only hope that these will forever satisfy the public hunger for Gilligan and company.

HEE HAW

THE GUILTY PARTIES

Creators:	Frank Peppiatt, John Aylesworth
Producers:	Frank Peppiatt, John Aylesworth, Sam Lovullo, Bill Davis
Directors:	Bill Davis, Bob Boatman
Writers:	Jack Burns, George Yanok, Archie Campbell, Gordie Tapp, Bud Wingard, Tom Lutz, Don Harron, Dave Cox
Tape Editors:	Marco Zappia, Sandy Lyles
Music Directors:	Don Rich, George Richey, Charlie McCoy
Animation by:	Format Productions

A Yongestreet Productions, Inc. production.

Starring Buck Owens and his Buckaroos and Roy Clark as hosts. Featuring Louis Marshall (Grandpa) Jones, David Akeman, Gordie Tapp, Sheb Wooley, Susan Raye, Archie Campbell, Lulu Roman, Jeannine Riley, Don Harron, Cathy Baker, The Hager Twins (Jon and Jim), Alvin "Junior" Samples, Jenifer Bishop, Minnie Pearl, Gunilla Hutton, Mary Taylor, Kathy Samples, Dianna Scott, Don Rich, Lisa Todd, Roni Stoneman, George Lindsey, Zella Lehr, Claude Phelps, Jimmy Riddle, Ann Randall, Misty Rowe, Mary Ann Gordon, Barbi Benton, Harry Cole, Gailard Sartain, Kenny Price, Cathy Barton, Buck Trent, Kingfish the Wonder Dog, Beauregard the Wonder Dog, and Buddy the Wonder Dog.

Debuted Sunday, June 15, 1969, 9 P.M. E.D.T. on CBS-TV.

THE FORMAT

"A rapid rural romp of retrogressive rejoinders distilled into idea-free, pure entertainment for America's tired brain," wrote Neil Hickey in *TV Guide*, trying to come up with a dignified definition for *Hee Haw*.

Others, TV critics mostly, tagged it as "tripe," "degrading," "vile," and "awful," claiming that "CBS ought to be ashamed." CBS might have been ashamed of the critical notices the program piled up, but certainly not of the high ratings it rolled up. The program, a cross between hayseed jokes and *Laugh-In,* was an unqualified hit from the beginning.

Each *Hee Haw* is composed of approximately 144 integrated cuts, or segments (the average variety show has about twenty segments), blending country music with cornball comedy. Hosts Roy Clark and Buck Owens, favorites among fans of country bumpkinism, front the proceedings and also take part in the sketches and offer their own musical interludes. Occasionally, these are special moments, as in the case of Clark's guitar rendition of "Malagueña." But most often we are subjected to such dubious musical favorites as "Who's Gonna Mow Your Grass?", "Your Squaw's On the Warpath," and "Hobo Meditations."

The program is most famous for its humor, or lack of it, and that is where the basic problem lies. Some gags on the show trace their ancestry back more than 100 years. The comic characters who deliver these highly "unforgettable" lines are no new inventions either. Dressed in overalls and tattered mountaineer miniskirts, á la Li'l Abner's Daisy Mae, they lounge around on haystacks or in rocking chairs to regale their audience with such thigh-slappers as:

"What are you doing carrying your wife's false teeth in your pocket?"

"I'm trying to keep her from eating between meals."

Or:

"Put out the cat!"

"Why? Is it on fire?"

Neither the gags nor the cornpone-fed characters are new and the production itself is old hat, having been lifted from *Laugh-In,* its predecessor and admitted show model. Instead of being doused by a bucket of water, one who tells a particularly bad joke on *Hee Haw*—and most of them are downright terrible—is hit over the head with a rubber chicken or slapped from the back by a swinging fence plank. An animated crow and talking donkey occasionally relieve their human counterparts by emoting such monstrosities as "Now don't that churn your butter?"

Like *Laugh-In, Hee Haw* has its set bits and, in fact, this is the show's stock in trade. Segments titled "The General Store," "The Moonshiners," "The Old Philosopher," "The Truck Stop," "Grandpa's Almanac," and "The Weather Girl" are so derivative and downright embarrassing that we wonder who actually enjoys them. Country comic favorites such as David Akeman who plays Stringbean are among the members of the resident company. They are augmented by appearances by such guest stars as Conway Twitty, Charley Pride, Loretta Lynn, Jerry Lee Lewis, Waylon Jennings, and Merle Haggard.

The show's "biggest" asset is a 300-pound "good ole boy" named Alvin "Junior" Samples. The former sawmill employee was plucked from the assembly line by producers Frank Peppiatt and John Aylesworth at the urging of Archie Campbell. Said *TV Guide*: "The importance of Mr. Samples to American Folklore is that—contrary to widespread opinion—he is *not* impersonating an inept, bumbling country comedian. He really *is* an inept, bumbling comedian. A modern Paul Bunyon, with real bunions!"

If *Hee Haw* sounds a bit manufactured—it is. Though backward in theme and tone, it is actually a slickly produced example of modern computer technology. A computer located in Los Angeles is used to organize and edit the seventy miles of videotape shot to fill out a season's segments. There goes the theory that computers are virtually infallible: one produces *Hee Haw*.

Year after corny year, *Hee Haw*'s ratings continue to rise. Apparently an awful lot of people think this show is funny . . . and that's not so funny.

FIVE *HEE HAW* PIG JOKES

The December 17, 1969, installment of *Hee Haw* featured a series of jokes dedicated to hogs. We reprint them here as samples of *Hee Haw* humor.

"This is National Swine Week. Take a pig to lunch."

"Did I hear you held your pigs up to the tree so they could eat apples off the branches one at a time? Don't you think that's an awful waste of time?"
"What's time to a pig?"

"Do you think we should bring the pigs in?"
"This house ain't fit for the pigs."

"What happened to the maid?"
"The pigs ate her."

"I'm sorry I ran over your hog, but you know I'll replace it."
"You know you're not near fat enough!"

SOME KIND WORDS FROM . . .

Ann Hodges of the *Houston Chronicle*:
"Possibly the worst [show] I've seen."

Eleanor Roberts of the *Boston Herald Traveler*:
"It's so bad, it's an insult to the intelligence of a nursery school dropout."

Martin Mayer in *About Television*:
"I was physically unable to watch for more than five minutes."

Cecil Smith of the *Los Angeles Times*:
"The most irrelevant, stupid and ghastly program in recent history."

This motley assemblage of Southern crackers is the cornpone Culhane family, one of the regular features of *Hee Haw*. Posing in the "drawing room" are (*l. to r.*) Gordie Tapp, Junior Samples, Grandpa Jones, and Lulu Roman.

Buck Owens and Roy Clark, the down-home Dan Rowan and Dick Martin, devote only three weeks a year taping their respective *Hee Haw* segments, due to some ingenious planning and schedule juggling. The pair performs separately around the country at fairs and in concert the rest of the year.

Buck Owens.

Archie Campbell, both *Hee Haw* performer and writer, has been with the show since its debut June 15, 1969.

Roy Clark.

Louis M. Jones, better known as Grandpa Jones, has been a legend among country cognoscenti for almost fifty years: "These are the same jokes I've been doing all my life."

Gordie Tapp, performer and writer.

Don Harron who plays Charlie, the disk jockey on the fictional KORN radio station, also writes part of the program's hillbilly humor: "I think it's the music more than the comedy that accounts for the series' success."

A *Hee Haw* highlight: Billy Carter dons special "Goober" overalls.

Gunilla Hutton and Dianna Scott. The former once said: "The really great thing about *Hee Haw* is that you get to play yourself, to use your own personality."

Buck Owens and Roy Clark celebrate the tenth anniversary of *Hee Haw*, proving that the so-called Silent Majority are anything but.

Buddy the Wonder Dog, a hillbilly Lassie, who replaced Kingfish the Wonder Dog and Beauregard the Wonder Dog in 1975.

FROM THE HORSE'S . . . (Roy Clark and Buck Owens)

Q. What does *Hee Haw* mean to you?
R. C.: It has no messages. It's not topical. And it's so fast-paced that if a joke fails, it doesn't hurt much because there's another coming right behind it.
B. O. We try to entertain all ages. We're not a hip show. We stay away from inside jokes as much as possible.

Q. Who is your audience?
R. C.. Sophisticated people see the show as a tremendous put-on and satire, and country people take it right at face value.
B. O. Anybody can grasp this material.

Q.: What has it really done for your careers?
R. C.: Because of the show, people recognize me now, even in swanky New York restaurants. I was in one recently when the headwaiter—a Hungarian fellow dressed in a tuxedo—came over to the table, leaned down and said, "Meeester Clark . . . As we say in my country—Heeeeee Haaaaaw!"

THE BUSINESS BEHIND THE BOX

Frank Peppiatt and John Aylesworth, a pair of Canadians who started their writing careers as copywriters at a Toronto ad agency in 1951, came to the U.S. to pursue their TV comedy writing ambitions. They lucked out with assignments for Perry Como, Judy Garland, Frank Sinatra, and Jonathan Winters. When the latter's CBS variety show was canceled in 1969, the duo, who also produced the Winters comedy hour, got to thinking: (1) that CBS's success in the ratings then was due in large part to the unexplained popularity of such down-home attractions as *The Beverly Hillbillies, Green Acres, Petticoat Junction,* and Glen Campbell's variety hour; and (2) that the ancient prevaudeville format of comedic blackouts done at a breakneck pace was in vogue, as witness the substantial success of *Laugh-In.*

Armed with these two known quantities, Peppiatt and Aylesworth put together a hasty prospectus for a series, titled it *Hee Haw,* and submitted it to Perry Lafferty, West Coast programing chief for CBS, who liked the idea enough to send it to Mike Dann, the network's senior vice president in charge of programing.

Operating from his thirty-fourth floor office at the New York headquarters of CBS, Dann was in the midst of locking up a summer schedule, particularly a warm weather replacement for *The Smothers Brothers Comedy Hour.* According to the brothers' contract with CBS, they had first crack at a thirteen-week summer replacement show, and their production company had in mind a show dealing with astrology, but Dann was not impressed. Exit the brothers Smothers for a summer vacation. Enter Perry Lafferty, whom Dann authorized to negotiate with Peppiatt and Aylesworth for *Hee Haw.*

With a firm contract to produce thirteen one-hour segments of their "outhouse *Laugh-In,*" as critic Cleveland Amory put it, the producers assembled a production staff of Hollywood veterans, including Bill Davis, director of Jonathan Winters' canceled show. Already lined up to front the show were Buck (Alvis Edgar) Owens, who had been voted America's #1 country music artist for five straight years, and his group, the Buckaroos (themselves esteemed as the #1 country band for four years), and roly-poly Roy Clark, twice national banjo champion before he was sixteen, voted Comedian of the Year by the Academy of Country and Western Music, clearly a favorite among the millions of country music aficionados.

For the next four weeks, cast and crew—some ninety people—worked at breakneck speed at the CBS affiliate, WLAC-TV, to videotape approximately 15,000 barnyard comedy bits and musical numbers, enough to fill out all thirteen shows, the first of which aired Sunday, June 15, 1969, in the Smothers Brothers' time slot, 9 P.M.

It was immediately perceived by "everybody" as a program of such stupefying banality, witlessness, and most of all pointlessness, that it immediately hit the top of the ratings, tying with *Laugh-In.* In fact, National Arbitron, one of the rating services, pegged it at 19.8 to its competition on NBC, *Bonanza's* 15.7.

Meant merely as a summertime trifle, *Hee Haw* was, for all intents and purposes, the biggest summer hit in the history of broadcasting, according to Mike Dann of CBS. "We're stuck with a hit," he said happily three weeks into the series run. "Too bad we can't keep it on the air come September." Dann, you see, had already promised that time slot to Leslie Uggams, having signed the singer to headline her own variety series (by this time, the Smothers Brothers were personae non grata at CBS). Immediately Dann negotiated with Peppiatt and Aylesworth to produce another passel of *Hee Haws* as a "revival," come midseason-replacement time in January, a case of stashing the corn in a deep freeze before serving.

Sure enough, by December Leslie Uggams was down the tube. But instead of replacing her with *Hee Haw*, as originally planned, Dann plopped Glen Campbell in her time slot and put *Hee Haw* in Campbell's Wednesday night spot. Why? Uggams' show had a predominantly black cast. To replace it with *Hee Haw*, a white show—a Southern white show, Dann reasoned—might have caused some racial strife. CBS had just recovered from enough travails with the Smothers Brothers; they didn't need other problems.

"We ran a year . . . until March of 1971," producer Aylesworth remembers. "Then CBS purged all the country shows [*Green Acres, The Beverly Hillbillies, Mayberry, R.F.D.,* etc.] and *Hee Haw* was swept out with the rest. Despite the fact the show was still in Nielsen's list of Top Ten programs, the network canned it anyway in favor of adopting a more urban image. "It was different for the other canceled shows," continues Aylesworth. "They were on film and could go into reruns in syndication. With *Hee Haw*, the only way we could go into syndication was to keep in production."

So Peppiatt and Aylesworth, doing business as Yongestreet Productions, bit the bullet and proceeded with their plans. They took out a big bank loan and mortgaged their homes to do the first thirteen syndicated shows, then offered the series on a station-by-station basis. By the time the first ratings sweep came in that November (1971), they had an impressive roster of 216 stations (the show now boasts 222 outlets) telecasting their country comedy. Thus *Hee Haw* not only survived but prevailed. In fact, it was doing so well, ABC wanted to buy it and put it back on a network. Yongestreet declined.

So now, twice a year, five weeks in the spring and another five in the fall, the *Hee Haw* gang assembles at station WTVF in Nashville to tape the syndie series—thirteen hour-long segments at a clip, to satisfy their 35 million fans, most of them living in rural areas of the U.S. and Canada.

What makes this turkey tick? Perhaps it is a classic case of something being so bad that it's good. There is not an ounce of originality evident. In fact, it appears that much of the writers' work must have come from researching the back pages of old *Grit* magazines or a dog-eared copy of *Captain Billy's Whiz Bang.*

Now, word has it, we can all look forward to a movie version of *Hee Haw.* Written by Peppiatt and Aylesworth and Jack Burns, the $6 million production is a comedy about a ninety-year-old New York millionaire who leaves his estate to the *Hee Haw* cast—and the attempts of a nephew to prevent them from getting the money. Director Bill Davis plans to use at least twenty-five famous screen villains. We can hardly wait.

HOGAN'S HEROES

THE GUILTY PARTIES

Creators:	Bernard Fein, Albert S. Ruddy
Producer:	Edward H. Feldman
Associate Producers:	Bernard Fein, William Calihan
Directors:	Robert Butler, Howard Morris, Gene Reynolds, Edward H. Feldman, Bruce Bilson, Marc Daniels, Robert Sweeney
Writers:	Richard M. Powell, Bernard Fein, Albert S. Ruddy, Laurence Marks, Phil Sharp, Harvey Bullock, Ray Allen, Arthur Julian, David Chandler, Jack H. Robinson
Music by:	Jerry Fielding
Casting:	Lynn Stalmaster, Irving Lande

A Bing Crosby Productions, Inc. production for CBS-TV.

Starring Bob Crane as Colonel Robert Hogan, Werner Klemperer as Colonel Wilhelm Klink, John Banner as Sergeant Hans Schultz, Robert Clary as Louis LeBeau, Richard Dawson as Peter Newkirk, Ivan Dixon as James Kinchloe, Larry Hovis as Andrew Carter, Cynthia Lynn as Helga, Sigrid Valdis as Hilda, Kenneth Washington as Richard Baker, and Leon Askin as General Alfred Burkhalter.

Debuted Friday, September 17, 1965, 8:30 P.M. E.D.T on CBS-TV.

THE FORMAT

Can life in a German prisoner of war camp be beautiful? It can be if your name is Colonel Robert Hogan (Bob Crane) and you're being held against your will in Stalag 13, an enemy camp from which no prisoner has ever escaped.

With enough contraptions and conveniences to make James Bond green with envy, the "heroes" manage to assist escaping Allied prisoners, sabotage Nazi bridges and factories, and channel secret information back to their intelligence headquarters in London. All of this, mind you, under the monocled eye of the camp commandant Wilhelm Klink (Werner Klemperer), a social climber who would think nothing of kissing the boot of a superior officer in order to gain a favor. His assistant, Sgt. Hans Schultz (John Banner) is a big dumb teddy bear with a weakness for chocolates and a penchant for muttering "I see nothing, . . . nothing" when confronted with the obvious disobedience of his prisoner charges.

The recalcitrant POW's include Louis LeBeau (Robert Clary), a stereotyped Frenchman who manages to whip up gourmet treats that would put Maxim's to shame; Corporal Peter Newkirk (Richard Dawson) who hails from Blighty with a deftness in communications; Sgt. Andrew Carter (Larry Hovis), all-American boy; and Corporal James Kinchloe (Ivan Dixon). Each is an ace in his field, ranging from demolitions to custom tailoring.

These Allied prisoners, led by Hogan, are always trying to escape. In fact, they have tunnels all over the camp, and a secret radio that operates twenty-four hours a day and, why, sometimes a couple of them just sneak out of the stalag and blow up a bridge and then sneak back in order to share a few guffaws with stupid Schultz. This is of course a distortion of history. Fact takes an awful beating here—Nazis were not lovable and they certainly were not stupid, and to portray these denizens of modern history as such is a terrible injustice. The Germans depicted in this show, could not have begun to threaten the entire European continent.

Wartime comedy can work effectively on television. Witness the success of *M*A*S*H*, another CBS sitcom. Unlike *Hogan's Heroes*, the *M*A*S*H* characters are vulnerable and human, whereas the idiots of Stalag 13 are no more than two-dimensional cartoon types—Nazi cartoon types to boot.

SOME KIND WORDS FROM ...

Jack Gould of the *New York Times*:
"... **Nazis as silly old buffoons, hopeless oafs who have more in common with Desilu Studios than Hitler.**"

Lawrence Laurent of the *Washington Post*:
"**[There is] not a Nazi in any form that ever existed. The Germans, conquerors of a continent, are played as lazy, doltish, cuddly, lovable, and cute.**"

Harlan Ellison of the *Los Angeles Free Press*:
"**It says Nazi prison camps are, at core, humorous places to spend a vacation.**"

Henry Mitchell of the *Memphis Commercial Appeal*:
"**I consider it distinctly sick.**"

The late Bob Crane (*center*) flanked by his costars John Banner (*left*) and Werner Klemperer. The sitcom actually registered some positive critical response: Frank Wilson of the Indianapolis *News* called it "... wild, completely unbelievable and fun," and Cynthia Lowry, writing for AP, said, "Maybe the little ones will be amused by the farce."

John Banner (*left*) plays a scene with Richard Dawson, today a popular game show host. Banner, a Jew, played the "cuddly" Schultz though he vehemently abhorred the term: "There is no such thing as a cuddly Nazi. I do not see Schultz as a Nazi at all; to me he represents some kind of goodness in any generation."

Werner Klemperer, who once played Adolf Eichmann in a quickie production called *Operation Eichmann*, was very vocal about the *Hogan's Heroes* setting: "I don't like people getting prisoner-of-war camps mixed up with concentration camps. You can't make fun of a concentration camp."

Despite the stark appearance of Stalag 13, the prisoners (*l. to r.*) Carter, Kinchloe, Newkirk, and LeBeau enjoyed Waldorf Astoria–like amenities like gourmet food, a barbershop with manicurist, a tailor shop, steambath, and printing facilities to produce phony money and passports. Not bad in the middle of wartime Deutschland.

Hogan himself, Bob Crane. The ex-disk jockey once played the next-door neighbor on *The Donna Reed Show.* He described *Hogan's* as "halfway between *Combat!* and *McHale's Navy*—with a little bit of *The Man from U.N.C.L.E.* thrown in."

THE BUSINESS BEHIND THE BOX

Against all odds—and *The Milton Berle Show*—CBS's Bilko series went on the air in the autumn of 1955. That spring, the show won the first of three consecutive Emmy Awards as "Best Comedy" series, plus a few more for its star Phil Silvers and its superior writing. The program now ranks among the handful of landmark TV sitcoms that have come and gone: *I Love Lucy, The Dick Van Dyke Show, All in the Family,* to name a few in the elite group.

A copy, no matter how carefully masked, was inevitable. What surprises us is that it took ten years to get on the air, and it almost didn't. "I tried for four years to sell the idea," says Bernard Fein, cocreator of the military sitcom. "Finally, I gave up and decided to leave the business altogether. I got on a plane headed for New York. Sitting next to me was a guy reading *Von Ryan's Express.* The minute I saw it, I said to myself, 'That's it!' "

Fein, once an actor—in fact, he played Private Gomez with Phil Silvers' merry men—had originally set his series in an American prison. It wasn't until the plane incident that he realized what the concept needed was a different setting. He got back on a plane bound for Los Angeles and, with collaborator Al Ruddy, turned out a new version of the script with a German POW camp locale.

"Four days after we finished it," recalls Fein, "Bing Crosby Productions bought it and CBS decided it was ready to proceed to pilot stage." The sample episode, titled "The Informer" and shot in black and white, set the pace for the remaining 167 episodes: Hogan and his men discover a German spy in the midst of their elaborate underground operation. Producer Edward H. Feldman, one time ad agency executive, peopled the pilot with one strong proven personality, Bob Crane, a seasoned radio disk jockey with two years' TV acting experience on *The Donna Reed Show*; he added Werner Klemperer, a German-born actor with a flair for comedy.

When the first Nielsens were posted for the two weeks ending September 26, 1965, *Hogan's Heroes* had placed #5, just ahead of *The Lucy Show* and *Andy Griffith,* making it the hit of the new season. "World War II with a laugh track" quipped one executive close to the show, while *Time,* in its official review, called it "a slapstick *Stalag 17.*"

Smelling a hit and assuming with good cause that the royalties from their play *Stalag 17* would diminish as a result of the week-in-week-out exploits of Hogan and his heroes, playwrights Donald Bevan and Edmund Trzcinski filed suit in Los Angeles Superior Court, claiming that *Hogan's Heroes* infringed on their copyright; that, indeed, "the story of a group of American prisoners lodged in a German prison camp" was the basis for the TV series. Naturally, the producers and creators of *Hogan's Heroes* vehemently denied using the play as a model, any more than they used Bilko as the basis, but the judge found in Bevan and Trzcinski's favor.

There were other ironies worth mentioning. Robert Clary, the actor who played the French gourmet LeBeau, was actually confined in Germany as a young man. Because of his Jewish ancestry, he spent years in Nazi concentration camps including Ottmuth, Blechhamer, Gross-Rosen, and the infamous Buchenwald. A grisly reminder, his prison number A-5717, is still tattooed on his upper left arm. On *Hogan's*, he whips up a batch of crêpes suzettes in a flash, but as an honest-to-goodness prisoner, one cup of water, called soup, was his ration—if he was lucky.

Although the name Robert Hogan was chosen by the show's creators and producer at random, and the fictional Stalag 13 could have been 14, or 15, or 16 (*never* 17), it turned up that there really *was* a Robert Hogan, a U.S. Army Air Force bomber pilot who was shot down over Germany during World War II, and captured and interned at the *real* Stalag 13, located in Nuremberg. Today, the real Hogan is a doctor living in Birmingham, Alabama. During the run of *Hogan's Heroes*, star Bob Crane journeyed to the South and had his picture taken with his real-life counterpart. It was good publicity to offset the plagiarism suit.

At the close of its first season, *Hogan's Heroes* ranked #9 in the Nielsens, an amazing feat for a fledgling show, just a rating point lower than both *Bewitched* and *The Beverly Hillbillies*, a pair of proven powerhouses. The question posed earlier in the season, "Who can laugh in a Nazi prison camp?" was now supplanted by a new query: "Why is it a success?"

Surprisingly, few viewers found any repulsive hangover memories about Nazism standing in the way of their enjoyment of *Hogan's Heroes*. Of course, this is partially true because the *Hogan's* audience was made up mostly of children (ages six to eleven) and teens (twelve to seventeen) according to all the surveys published in *Television* magazine. They were of a generation too young to remember the horrors of World War II or care too much about it. That, in itself, is a shame. To think that *Hogan's Heroes* has been the first introduction to World War II for many millions of impressionable youngsters is appalling. These silly Nazis were nothing like the genuine articles. It's like trying to pass off Soupy Sales as a nuclear scientist.

The show was a hit, too, in England, France, Australia, Japan, the Philippines, Holland, and South America. Japan, in fact, classified the show as a "documentary" in pre-airing publicity, and in Tokyo the series was Top Ten stuff. (No overseas sale was effected in West Germany, we might add.)

Although, during its second year the show ranked #18 among all shows—a very respectable placement indeed—CBS thereafter tampered with the time slot, moving it around at will until it finally wound up on Sunday evenings as Ed Sullivan's lead-in at 7:30 P.M. It was finally dropped in 1971 after six years on the air, along with Sullivan, *Hee Haw*, and a long list of CBS favorites.

"If you liked World War II," said Bob Crane early on, "you'll love *Hogan's Heroes*." As for us, we weren't crazy about either of them.

JACKPOT BOWLING STARRING MILTON BERLE

THE GUILTY PARTIES

Producer:	Buddy Arnold
Associate Producer:	Hal Collins
Director:	Dave Brown
Sponsors:	Phillies Cigars, the Brunswick Corporation

Starring Milton Berle as host and Chick Hearn as announcer.
Debuted Monday, September 19, 1960, 10:30 P.M. E.D.T. on NBC-TV.

THE FORMAT

"When a man sends a bowling ball down the alley," *TV Guide*'s Mel Durslag remarked, "one of two things happens: (a) It knocks down the pins, or (b) it doesn't. It is a bloodless spectacle, hardly evoking suspense or producing spasms of delight."

The problem, then, confronting *Jackpot Bowling Starring Milton Berle* was what to do to alleviate the enormous boredom that results from watching balls rolling down lanes. The solution, or so the sponsors reasoned, was to bring in Milton Berle for "comedy relief." But as Milton himself joked on the first broadcast: "Twenty-one minutes of bowling and nine minutes of Milton Berle. Nine minutes! I usually bow that long!"

Getting serious in an interview with Don Page of the *Los Angeles Times*, Uncle Miltie emphasized, "This is not my show. The bowling comes first. My part is to integrate comedy and make it more of an entertainment show rather than a show designed for sports fans only." But *Jackpot Bowling* was, first and foremost, a bowling show. Attempting to inject humor between strikes and spares did not work. No matter what, all that remained were bowling balls and the deafening crash of pins.

For "Always Leave 'Em Laughing" Berle, this oil-and-water dilemma caused some obvious problems. "I never know what will happen next," he offered in a 1960 newspaper interview. "I'm supposed to have one minute and forty-five seconds for my opening. That means about nine jokes if I talk fast. I talk fast. Between the matches, I'm supposed to plan for four and a half minutes but if the matches run long, I have to cut right on the air." When producer Buddy Arnold, sitting nervously on the sidelines with a stopwatch, signaled Milton to cut, he had to cut. This sort of regimen is like removing one of the comic's arms. Added to that, plainly and simply—bowling needed Berle like a hole in the head pin.

Each telecast begins with two professional bowlers competing in a nine-frame match in which only strikes count. The premiere show featured Don Carter and Ray Bluth (who lost). The winner receives $1,000. If, perchance, the bowler has a string of six successive strikes during the competition, he receives a bonus of $5,000. The winner is also entitled to meet another pro in the second match of the evening. On the opener, this was Harry Smith. First prize in this, too, is $1,000, but the bonus for six straight strikes increases sharply to a minimum of $25,000. Each week that the jackpot—hence the title of the show—isn't won, the pot is sweetened by $5,000.

Of course, the odds against one's rolling six straight strikes are astronomical, but by the October 10 show, Frank Clause had done it, claiming the $40,000 purse. For the bowlers privileged enough to appear on the show, *Jackpot Bowling* was an excellent arrangement (even the losers received $250). But as a spectator sport, the pastime does nothing to excite an audience. It is, in short, mostly a participant's sport. Because of this, the job of "animating" the games became a sticky affair for Chick Hearn, who was used to broadcasting such vigorous sports as football, basketball, and horse racing. It was like giving a play-by-play for a game of tiddlywinks.

To add a little entertainment value to the proceedings, a show business celebrity bowled for his favorite charity between the two formal matches. Steve Allen and Desi Arnaz, among others, did the honors, but this hardly raised the show above its own mediocrity, a situation clearly caused by mingling Milton Berle with bowling.

BERLE'S BOWLING BAG OF GAGS

Can a bowling ball find happiness with an automatic pinsetter?

This season you have Milton Berle and bowling. Last season it was Jack Paar and bawling.

I'm doing this for "pin" money.

I hope people will refer to the game now as "Berle-ing."

Fan mail generated by *Jackpot Bowling* fell into two categories: (1) "How dare those bowlers take up so much time?" and (2) "What do we need Berle for?"

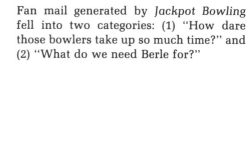

Uncle Miltie on *Jackpot Bowling*: "We've taken bowling out of the pool room class and made it more appealing. This way we're attracting a good cross section of viewers and showing them that bowlers are great athletes and what a fine game bowling is."

SOME KIND WORDS FROM...

Melvin Durslag of *TV Guide:*
"A monumental bore.... The overall product is a mongrel which leaves the viewer grossly unsatisfied."

Tedd Thomey in *The Glorious Decade:*
"A horrible mishmash."

The *New York Times:*
"The bowling was desultory...."

There was no way "Mr. Tuesday Night" could become "Mr. Monday Night" with a show like *Jackpot Bowling.* "I'm not worried about television critics," Berle said. "You want to know the Berle philosophy? It's breathing." Too bad there was little life in *Jackpot Bowling.*

THE BUSINESS BEHIND THE BOX

"People wonder what I'm doing on this show," quipped Milton Berle on opening night of *Jackpot Bowling.* "I'll tell you. The sponsor called me up—and I said: 'I'll take it!'"

What "Mr. Television" took was $15,000 a week from sponsor Bayuk Cigars, makers of Phillies, a tidy sum indeed to play stooge to a row of tenpins; an assignment, mind you, that required no more than nine minutes of performance every Monday night starting September 19, 1960.

Why did Milton Berle, TV's erstwhile "Mr. Tuesday Night," agree to host a run-of-the-mill bowling show? "The sponsor wanted an offbeat dimension," explained Berle, TV's own kingpin of the 1940s and early 1950s, "a standup comedian in a sports show who could squeeze laughs into 120-second segments."

Prior to Berle's association with *Jackpot Bowling,* the show had enjoyed a three-year run on NBC. Used solely to fill the time between the conclusion of the match on *Cavalcade of Sports* and the start of the 11 P.M. local news, the show ran through a series of hosts such as Leo Durocher, Mel Allen, and Bud Palmer, none of whom had the slightest affiliation with bowling. Promised a full half-hour slot for the 1960-61 season by NBC, sponsor Phillies decided to jazz up the offering by having Uncle Miltie around.

After performing in more than 400 live, hour-long TV shows since his debut on *The Texaco Star Theatre* back in 1948, Berle decided it was time to take it easier: "I didn't want the headaches of a comedy series or specials, and by then I didn't have to prove I was funny. I did *Jackpot* just to keep my hand in.''

Aside from his weekly salary as host, Berle was on the receiving end of a $100,000-a-year stipend from NBC, the result of the celebrated thirty-year contract he signed with the web in 1951. It naturally behooved NBC to keep its high-priced "name" working to get something back on his salary, which called for an increase of $2,500 per show each season, plus one-third ownership in the series. "Who needs it?" Berle once asked himself. "Uncle Miltie makes it, Uncle Sam takes it.''

Berle didn't want to get that involved in the production of the show, as he had during his nine years of weekly live shows. "It's a snap," Berle commented about *Jackpot Bowling* at the time. "The show goes live from Hollywood at seven-thirty. I come in half an hour before air time. My producer's lined up the bowlers. My director's rehearsed the five camers. He points to where I stand. I do an opening monologue and introduce Chick Hearn. Then I come back between matches, maybe a minute, maybe four minutes, depending on how long the play lasts. Then I say good night and close the show. At eight o'clock I put on my hat and I go home.''

And he added: "No cast. No guests. No script. No ulcers. Just a camera, cut to your host, Milton Berle, and then back to the bowling.''

Berle enjoyed giving the impression that he strolled into the Hollywood Legion Lanes a few minutes before show time, lit up one of his sponsor's cigars, and rattled off a few jokes. Actually, he arrived early every Monday morning, conferred with his four writers (although he often claimed everything was ad-libbed), rehearsed the actors with their lines, including the "spontaneous" remarks some of them were to make to him from the bowling crowd, etc., etc., etc. It was quite an undertaking for the man who said, "I'm not going to kill myself again. I'm happy with a bowling show.''

The "bowling show" was equally happy with Berle. Despite some keen competition from ABC's stylish *Peter Gunn* series, *Jackpot Bowling* racked up some impressive ratings. But by March 13, 1961, Berle's contract with the cigar makers had run out. Insiders predicted that the Brunswick people, manufacturers of the bowling alley equipment, would take over sole sponsorship, but this didn't materialize.

Whatever the case, it was a prudent decision Miltie made to bow out gracefully, allowing the show a dignified death. *Jackpot Bowling* was a bowling show, pure and simple. Milton Berle did not belong anymore than the Pope belonged on *Laugh-In*. Perhaps two of Berle's best buddies said it all via jokes: "Milton," said George Burns, "only you would have the nerve to stand in a bowling alley and tell jokes!" Steve Allen, asked by Berle why he wasn't hosting a game show, answered: "It isn't because I haven't got the talent. I haven't got the guts.''

THE
JERRY LEWIS
SHOW

THE GUILTY PARTIES

Executive Producer:	Ernest D. Glucksman
Producer:	Perry Cross
Associate Producer:	Mack Bing
Director:	John Dorsey
Writers:	Bob Howard, Bill Richmond,
	Dick Cavett, Jerry Lewis
Makeup by:	Jack Stone
Musical Director:	Lou Brown

A Jerry Lewis Enterprises production for ABC-TV.
    Starring Jerry Lewis, with Del Moore as announcer.
    Debuted Saturday, September 21, 1963, 9:30 P.M. E.D.T. on ABC-TV.

THE FORMAT

It sounded pretty promising, if you listened to Jerry Lewis: "I can now do television the way I want to do it. I have something to say, something to show; I have something to do, and I have that God-given gift of communicating with people. And that's what I'm going to do for two hours on Saturday nights. I often do it anyhow, for more than two hours, with friends and even sometimes with strangers. On the show I'm gonna not do any more than let the camera in on it. In the middle of a discussion, I may dance, or jump up and down, or do a gag. I'll have guests. I'll have big instrumentation. I'll be communicating and I'll be giving people something they've never been able to buy in a nightclub or purchase a ticket for at any box office."

The Last Supper, with the original cast, would have had trouble living up to that one. And, like his mortal self, his show, aptly named *The Jerry Lewis Show*, never rose above the level of basic mediocrity, and it's easy to understand why.

Jerry Lewis is a comedian. His many films—at least those made prior to the mid-1960s—made him a millionaire. Like Chaplin and a few others, he enjoys a cultlike following in some countries, particularly France. In America, many view Mr. Lewis a bit differently. His motion pictures are now considered old-hat and pointless, his appearances on talk shows are, more often than not, grating on the nerves, and his only current claim to fame is that of host and mentor of an annual telethon.

The idea of his monopolizing two hours of prime air-time is an appalling thought, but that's exactly what happened during the fall of 1963 over ABC-TV. "Total control and autonomy" were what Jerry wanted and got, and he managed to use these privileges to the detriment of his own TV program.

Take the first show, for instance. The guest list, prepared by Lewis himself, included the likes of Mort Sahl, Clifton Fadiman, and Kay Stevens. (He *wanted* Count Basie and Cardinal Spellman. He tried to get Jonas Salk, claiming, "I wanted to ask him what he does.")

As expected, the show relied far too much on Lewis' antics—his screeches, his tongue waggings, his eye crossings, his "Leonard baby" references to the man who "hired" him, ABC's Leonard Goldenson. His patter was forgettable and deadly, like the lengthy discussion of how there should be less attention paid to the old rule of not identifying other networks. And every once in a while, some unexpected guest would enter through an upstage door, like Steve Allen, Jimmy Durante, or Bob Stack, whose *Untouchables* had just left ABC. Even Johnny Carson, about to celebrate his first anniversary on the *Tonight* show, phoned Lewis from New York to welcome him back to television.

As the weeks went on, Lewis became more tense, more serious, and less the Jerry Lewis that his fans—some of whom were possibly still watching—came to expect. Toward the end of the show's thirteen-week run, he immersed himself in a bath of self-pity and paranoia. Spotting a priest in the audience one night, he said, "Father, would you like to give me the last rites?"

He took the closing moments of the last show in December to pin the rap for his failure on ABC and the sponsors. He didn't need television, he said.

A few years later, he returned to the medium (he didn't need) in a structured variety format, hoping to capture some of the success his ex-partner, Dean Martin, had already achieved. That never happened, and, to this day, Jerry Lewis remains bitter about his failure.

MEMORABLE MOMENTS

?!!

Two years after wounds healed, Jerry Lewis had this to say about TV: "I have no desire to get back into television. It's dull. It's canned. It's tasteless. It's been swallowed up by Madison Avenue. Right after the dinner hour, we hear all about underarm deodorants, bad breath, and loose dentures. It's disgusting."

Lewis took another crack at television in 1967, this time for NBC. It was a structured, fully scripted variety show. Still, he had excuses to offer about his earlier ABC fiasco: "I tried to do all the steering because I was surrounded by incompetence."

THE JERRY LEWIS SHOW

On his swan-song telecast, December 21, 1963, Lewis admitted, "I didn't play the game their way. I'm a nonconformist and I didn't adhere to certain rules and regulations. I just don't like to do like I'm supposed to."

"Two hours," Lewis said at the top of the first show, "is a big lot of time." It was, indeed, and though he made a point of the fact that much of the show was unrehearsed, it seemed it would have been far better to go along with the gag that it was *all* unrehearsed.

SOME KIND WORDS FROM ...

Cleveland Amory of *TV Guide:*
"The Jerry Lewis Show **is live—but not by much. . . ."**

Jack Gould of the *New York Times:*
"Patent gracelessness, . . . a telethon of vapidity. The star needs instruction in remedial conversation. . . ."

Time magazine:
"[Do] several million people want to watch 120 minutes of the scriptless life of a semi-educated egocentric boor?"

The idea of *The Jerry Lewis Show* was to combine "entertainment and serious stuff, like the *Tonight* show." Lewis's press agent, Jack Keller, offered these show possibilities: Helen Keller and the Wiere Brothers; Albert Schweitzer and Blackstone the Magician; Eileen Farrell singing with Spike Jones, with guest stars Khrushchev and Billy Graham.

THE BUSINESS BEHIND THE BOX

Were it not for Jack Paar's festering disenchantment with television back in 1962, we might have been spared the agony of *The Jerry Lewis Show.* When Paar announced his resignation from the *Tonight* show, NBC wasted no time in signing up a thirty-seven-year-old comedian and game show host by the name of Johnny Carson to replace him. Carson, however, had a contract with *Who Do You Trust?* producer Don Fedderson which forced the comic to remain with the quiz show until the fall of 1962, which left the *Tonight* people without a star for six months. Guest hosts filled in, including Art Linkletter, Joey Bishop, Soupy Sales, Mort Sahl, and Jerry Lewis.

The *Tonight* audience, some 8 million strong, was astonished that Lewis, known strictly for his slapstick comedy routines, could suddenly switch from insanity to serious discussion. One viewer wrote, "I never knew he could converse." Jerry surprised not only viewers by his verbal deftness, but also network officials, sponsors, and critics, even those usually prone to putting down his films. He was funny, his ad-libbing was in good taste, he was adept at interviewing a wide range of guests, and he could hawk the sponsors' wares. The power people were beginning to think in terms of a regular show for the comedian.

"NBC and CBS rammed heads over me," Lewis was quoted in a *TV Guide* article in the spring of 1963. "Jim Aubrey, head of CBS—they didn't send no *boys*—came out and said, 'Name the figure for a show.' That was for openers. He said, 'Look, we got Judy Garland and Danny Kaye, and we'll drop you in the middle.' I said, 'So I wind up part of the package? That's very, very good for CBS, but forget it. I'm not gonna be in no middle.'

" 'Now you'll hear *my* terms,' I told him. 'I won't do sixty minutes.' He said, 'An awful lot of people do sixty minutes . . .'

"I said, 'I'm not an awful lot of people, Jim. I am this big, handsome, popular young Jewish movie star, and I'm not going to prepare a lot of ha-ha-ha for five days until it's comin' outta my ears.'

"I said, 'I want to go on when I'm ready, right then, when I feel like it, so people will push the button and it will happen for them *now,* like television ought to be, no pre-recording, no tape, no delayed broadcast . . . it *happens.'*

" 'Besides,' I told him, 'sixty minutes is not enough. For the kind of loot you got to pay me you'll need four boys to sponsor sixty minutes of that kind of money.'

"I said, 'I got to have complete autonomy over who my sponsors will be. I will not hold up a product I think is phony. And I will not impose on my audience underarm deodorant, mouthwash, athlete's foot preparations, or anything distasteful.'

"He said, 'Come on . . .'

"I said, 'Therefore, I will not settle for less than the title of the show: *Madhouse 90.'*

"He said, 'Oh, Lord, I don't know where we'll get ninety minutes.'

"I said, 'Is that all you're worried about? The meeting is over.' "

Aubrey departed, and a week later, in waltzed Mort Werner, head programing honcho for NBC. He said his network was prepared to give Lewis his ninety minutes, either on Tuesday or Thursday nights.

"Forget it," said Lewis. "I ain't going on in no middle of the week. People are gonna make dates for Saturday night to see my show."

Werner said, "We just spent millions for movies on Saturday nights."

"Good luck to you *and* your movies, Mr. Werner," Jerry intoned. "Enjoy 'em."

Mort Werner departed.

A few months later, Jerry's executive producer, Ernest D. Glucksman, informed the comic that now ABC was interested in making an offer. Busy editing *The Nutty Professor,* Lewis had just about lost interest in doing a television show. "Jerry," Ernie pleaded, "they're talking astronomical figures."

Enter Leonard Goldenson, head of ABC: "Tell us what you want, Jerry, and you got it."

"I want Saturday night for two hours. I'm stealing thirty minutes because I figure you'll finger me for thirty of the ninety I want at least—so I'll wind up with ninety anyhow."

"If you want two hours, you've got them," Goldenson conceded.

"Saturday night, ten to twelve," Lewis insisted. "Also complete autonomy over the program and commercials, for forty shows a year for five years."

"You're talking about more money than we own," the ABC mogul hinted.

Lewis then generously gave Goldenson one hour to make up his mind. The contract Jerry was asking for amounted to $14 million a year, or about $72 million for five seasons. It constituted the biggest deal ever negotiated for a single performer's services. It was not an easy decision for the ABC chieftain to make. His network was just winding down from one of the most disastrous seasons in its history, with plans to put seventeen new shows on the fall 1963 schedule, among them *Burke's Law, The Farmer's Daughter,* and *The Fugitive.*

On April 22, the network made the official announcement: *The Jerry Lewis Show* would be a two-hour *live* foray every Saturday night from 9:30 to 11:30, "a free-form design to afford Jerry all the leeway he needs for his unconfined and high-comedy style, with no stopwatches on any phase of the performance. . . . No two shows will be alike." The "spontaneous" program would be a veritable "open house for celebrities, a landmark" in television entertainment.

The show was to feature variety and conversation, with big-name bands and such oddly mixed guests as Cardinal Spellman and Peggy Lee. "The Grand Mogul of the Muggers," as *TV Guide* dubbed Lewis, added: "It's going to be the only show in television where there will be no pre-recording, not even to the degree of one pre-recorded line. All the commercials, everything will be live: the guests, the interviews, the acts, *everything, everybody* . . . all live."

Lewis insisted on a "glamorous" setting for the show and production values to match, so ABC bought the El Capitan Theatre on Vine Street in Hollywood; totally refurbished the one-time legitimate theater at an estimated cost of $1 million, according to Jerry's specifications; and renamed it accordingly—the Jerry Lewis Theatre.

On "opening night"—Lewis intended *every* program as a theatrical "event," right down to assigned seats for the 800-strong audience—September 21, 1963, the star was justifiably nervous. The theater renovation had been barely completed, the communications system, linking cameramen to the director in the booth, was not working, and the huge, ten-by-twelve-foot screen above the stage, put there so the audience could get a clear view of the goings-on, was black, with no sign of showing *anything* live that night, much less the new *Jerry Lewis Show*.

Nevertheless, at 6:30 P.M. (West Coast time), Lou Brown's orchestra struck up the theme song and Del Moore hyped into his mike: "And here he is—Jerry Lewis *live* from Hollywood!"

For the next two hours, Lewis and 172 crew members tried valiantly to make it come together. So did guests Mort Sahl, Steve Allen, Jimmy Durante, Kay Stevens, and Harry James and his band. In addition to his hosting chores, Jerry took part in an "improvised" sketch with Joyce Jameson, Milton Frome, and Jesse White, but it fell flatter than Jerry's musical tribute to little girls, "Think Pink." The one ray of hope was his introduction of a massive Adonis as "the winner of the Jerry Lewis look-alike contest." But one four-minute bit does not a two-hour marathon make.

The much-heralded, overpublicized *Jerry Lewis Show* started out understandably high in the ratings, but by the second show, Lewis' audience had diminished by 50 percent, this despite some "sure-fire" guests like Liberace, Ruby Keeler, and Jack Jones. This sad turn of events obviously concerned the mighty ABC. Lewis himself had joked on the opener: "We're just having fun here . . . for a fortune!" Now the network insisted on taking over some control of their fun-for-a-fortune program. They wanted a "set" format—no more "free-wheeling spontaneity"—and a firm script.

This demand enraged Lewis, who had insisted on complete autonomy. It touched off a running feud between Jerry and ABC and the sponsors that culminated with the announcement on November 19: "Despite a firm, forty-week commitment, [ABC] has granted Lewis' request to withdraw the show due to extreme differences of opinion regarding its format."

ABC settled with Lewis to the tune of some $4 million, although other sources claim the amount was something closer to $750,000. What the network had hoped would be "a milestone of television entertainment" turned out instead to be a different sort of landmark—the most monumental flop in the history of the medium.

LAND OF THE GIANTS

THE GUILTY PARTIES

Creator/Producer:	Irwin Allen
Associate Producer:	Jerry Briskin
Directors:	Harry Harris, Sobey Martin, Irwin Allen, Nathan H. Juran, Harmon Jones, et al.
Writers:	Dan Ullman, Anthony Wilson, Jack Turley, Mann Rubin, Peter Packer, Arthur Weiss, et al.
Cameraman:	Howard Schwartz
Art Directors:	Jack Martin Smith, Rodger E. Maus
Music by:	Lionel Williams, John Williams

An Irwin Allen Production in association with Kent Productions, Inc. and 20th Century-Fox Television for ABC-TV.

Starring Gary Conway as Steve Burton, Kurt Kasznar as Alexander Fitzhugh, Don Marshall as Dan Erickson, Heather Young as Betty Hamilton, Don Matheson as Mark Wilson, Deanna Lund as Valerie Scott, and Stefan Arngrim as Barry Lockridge.

Debuted Sunday, September 22, 1968, 7 P.M. E.D.T. on ABC-TV.

THE FORMAT

Question: In what TV series did alley cats and Hoover vacuum cleaners serve as villains? If you guessed *Land of the Giants,* you win first prize in the Irwin Allen Sweepstakes—a free adventure on the S. S. *Poseidon.*

It's June 12, 1983, and the *Spinthrift,* suborbital flight 612, en route from New

York to London, encounters a strange and violent turbulence. The chartered craft is practically out of control when the crew spies a city below, which they assume is Blighty. A quick swerve prevents a head-on crash into an office building—but how can this be?—the altimeter registers 30,000 feet.

An amazing emergency landing is effected before Captain Steve Burton (Gary Conway) and copilot Dan Erickson (Don Marshall) embark on an exploratory expedition. Suddenly two large headlights cut through the dense fog and a huge automobile passes directly over them! It takes no more clues: they are not in merry ole England—in fact, they are not on Earth.

Some amazing "space warp," caused by a planet experimenting with space probes, has sucked them in like a mammoth magnet. The environs resemble Earth in many ways except everything is twelve times larger than normal—by Earth standards, that is. Men stand seventy-two feet tall, a cat is the size of Disney's Dumbo, and a john could hold an entire navy of Tidy Bowl men.

Steve and Dan, two men in a brave new world (minus Huxley), return to their spacecraft only to learn that a giant little boy has discovered them and is playing with the plane, as if it were a new Hot Wheels model. The two manage to escape in the plane by using a new, untapped energy source, and find themselves in a thick forest inhabited by a litter of pussy cats, who damage the craft beyond repair.

Captain Steve is responsible for the safety of not only his crew—co-pilot Erickson and sexy stewardess Betty Hamilton (Heather Young)—but also the four passengers on board: a millionaire, Mark Wilson (Don Matheson) who's beside himself because he'll lose $50 million if he can't get back to London before the banks close; a jet-setter, Valerie Scott (Deanna Lund) who spends considerable time bitching about missing the comforts of home; a boy, Barry Lockridge (Stefan Arngrim) who's an orphan and his dog Chipper; and last, but definitely not least, Commander Alexander Fitzhugh (Kurt Kasznar) who, in fact, is a professional con man in naval uniform. (Good going, Irwin Allen—you included every cliché character in the book.)

"These are real people and their emotions are real," Gary Conway insists. "I've never met the people they have on most TV shows. Our show was science fiction with an identifiable base. Realistic fantasy . . ."

Harlan Ellison, author of umpteen books of science fiction and something of a recognized authority on the subject, had a different viewpoint: "To a physiologist, the giantism of *Land of the Giants* is laughable. It ignores the inverse cube law. It can't be. It never could be. But kids all over this country liked the show, and after a while you were willing to suspend disbelief to enjoy the stories. That is, you *would* be willing to do so were not the plots so stupid and boring."

MEMORABLE MOMENTS

- Mistakenly believing that they are back on Earth, the travelers are trapped in a "human-sized" village, where they become the playthings of a giant inventor and his sadistic grandchild.

- The travelers are captured by a sinister gypsy who plans to feature them in his carnival. Preventing their escape—a vicious trained bear.

- Amnesia victim Fitzhugh is captured by giant thieves who persuade him to join their scheme to steal a priceless ruby.

- Mark is lured into danger by a beautiful, sirenlike girl—an earthling whose home is with the giants.

SOME KIND WORDS FROM ...

Cleveland Amory of *TV Guide*:
"All in all, if you're under eleven, you're bound to enjoy this show. If you're over eleven, lots of luck."

Rex Reed:
"... looks like it was written in thirty minutes over a pastrami sandwich ..."

Harlan Ellison of the Los Angeles *Free Press*:
"The stupidity, vapidity, and eczema-producing banality of this most recent Irwin Allen monstrosity has brought a wince to anyone remotely familiar with science fiction."

Gary Conway, star of *Giants*: "TV is too damned talky, and with nothing to say—it's pretty bad."

(*top*) Don Matheson played millionaire Mark Wilson, one of the *Spinthrift* passengers who finds himself stranded on a strange planet inhabited by giants. Matheson had appeared in Irwin Allen's other series, *Voyage to the Bottom of the Sea* and *Lost in Space,* another winner.

(*center*) A guest role in ABC's *Batman* led actress Deanna Lund to a part in Frank Sinatra's *Tony Rome* film. Twentieth Century-Fox quickly signed her to a long-term contract just prior to her being inked as the femme lead in *Giants*. Recently, Ms. Lund was a production assistant on a syndicated game show.

(*below*) Young Stefan Arngrim, as orphaned Barry Lockridge, confronts the villain, Alexander Fitzhugh, played by Broadwayite Kurt Kasznar, in "The Trap," the third episode of *Land of the Giants* to be filmed.

(*left*) Don Marshall essayed the role of the copilot Dan Erickson in Irwin Allen's gargantuan travesty, *Land of the Giants*. (*right*) Stewardess Betty Hamilton was played by lovely Heather Young about whom Cleveland Amory quipped in *TV Guide:* "She's a terrific morale booster in spite of the fact that in addition to sharing all the troubles the others have, she also is almost constantly strangled by her size-one sweater."

THE BUSINESS BEHIND THE BOX

Best known today for pioneering the so-called "disaster" flicks like *The Towering Inferno* and *The Poseidon Adventure*, Irwin Allen spent his prior years producing a spate of TV adventure series—innocuous bits of fluff like *Lost in Space*, *Voyage to the Bottom of the Sea*, *The Time Tunnel*. With this trio of TV programs securely under his belt, the former disk jockey proceeded to concoct a little number titled *Land of the Giants*.

With rare foresight, ABC bought *Giants* in the summer of 1967, intending to use it as a midseason replacement show in the event that one of its fall series bombed. Even though those troubles predictably developed, ABC executives were so overwhelmed with the *Land of the Giants* segments already filmed that they decided to withhold them until the following fall. They smelled a winner, or so they thought.

The brilliant concept of transporting a heterogeneous group of air travelers into a world inhabited by giants was not a new idea. Back in 1959, CBS bought thirteen episodes of a Ziv-produced series titled *World of the Giants*, starring Marshall Thompson as a six-inch "hero" who works for a super-secret government agency. His normal-sized colleague, played by Arthur Franz, carried him around in a specially fitted attaché case equipped with a bucket seat and safety belt. James Aubrey of CBS wisely never put the show on his network, instead selling the baker's-dozen package to United Artists for syndication.

Whether Irwin Allen got his inspiration from the earlier effort is immaterial. An astute businessman as well as a proficient producer, Allen acknowledges: "I do these shows for money. The idea originated from a personal dream. My dreams are wild and woolly. My subconscious forces these dreams on me, and I have the most commercial subconscious in town! Even my dreams have commercials."

Gary Conway, who toplined *Giants,* described the series as a "modern day *Gulliver's Travels.*" Conway was known to television audiences for having played Gene Barry's aide, Tim Tilson, in the 1966 detective series *Burke's Law. Giants* was a radical departure for the actor, who admitted that "I was very anti-science fiction on TV." An accomplished artist, Conway must have done *Giants* purely for money. In fact, during production, he commented: "There is a lot of indifference on the set. Some are here for psychological reasons, others are in it for the money."

Every series has its "heavy" and *Giants* had Kurt Kasznar, a refugee from the Broadway stage. Vienna-born Kasznar cut his theatrical teeth as an Army training-film director, moved on to New York to create the roles of Uncle Max in *The Sound of Music* and Victor Velasco in Neil Simon's *Barefoot in the Park.* He did the *Giants* pilot as a lark, not expecting it to sell. Kasznar is guarded about his association with the series: "I respect the show. I reached a public I never reached before. I'm glad I did not get billed above the title, though. Then people think you're somehow responsible."

The series was unveiled on Sunday, September 22, 1968, pitted against NBC's super-popular Disney hour and on CBS a new kid's show, *Gentle Ben,* and the long running *Lassie. Giants* found its audience among young people and a lot of women over thirty-five, prompting Irwin Allen to quip, "I guess women are fond of giants." (The females in question were probably just wornout moms whose viewing habits were dictated by their school-age kids.)

At a per-episode cost of $250,000, *Land of the Giants* was at that time TV's most expensive hour. The company utilized two sprawling soundstages at Twentieth Century-Fox's huge lot in West Los Angeles. Bill Abbott, the well-known optical genius and photography magician, had his work cut out for him trying to transform automobiles into sixty-foot monsters, making pencils appear to be three feet long and telephones four feet high. This often caused problems. The giants were supposed to be twelve times the size of the "little" people.

Giants lasted two seasons. It was replaced by one of those so-called "relevant" shows of 1970, *The Young Rebels,* which lasted all of fifteen weeks. Failure at that hour on Sunday is forever blamed on Disney. "Good movies draw because they grab them by the guts," said *Giants* star Gary Conway. "In TV, people don't want to strive for greatness. Most start with a limited goal."

The defense rests.

THE LIBERACE SHOW

THE GUILTY PARTIES

Producer: Don Fedderson
Director: Duke Goldstone
Musical Director: George Liberace

Starring Liberace.
Debuted Tuesday, July 1, 1952, 7:30 P.M. E.D.T. on NBC-TV.

THE FORMAT

You are ushered into a handsome but antiseptic living room. The lighting is managed so that you see a figure in silhouette poised over a keyboard. The piano, a concert grand, is a Baldwin.

An unseen orchestra, led by George Liberace, throbs emotionally as a soft background to the finely manicured hands moving across the keys in the opening theme music. Your eye begins to catch more details of the picture, and it falls on the candelabra, a gaudy five-branched affair standing in solitude on the piano to the performer's left. The camera glides toward the pianist and the lights come up gradually. You are almost face to face with him. His head is bent over the instrument, and you can sense his dedication. Slowly he lifts his head, and the smooth handsome face of a man in his early thirties is welcoming you into his home. He winks his eye ever so meaningfully and you feel you have been accepted into the inner circle.

Wearing white shoes, white socks, white pants, white coat, white shirt, white tie, and white teeth, the man named Liberace greets his audience, the home viewer. He explains that his sponsor, a tuna fish packer, has given him lots of cases of the product and if any of the mothers "out there in TV-land" have new tuna recipes, send them to his mother in the San Fernando Valley.

Now we are ready for the first big production number. It might be "The Skater's Waltz," and here's where you get a chance to watch Lee's (that's what his friends call him) hands at the keyboard. Your eyes are drawn at once to the ring on his right pinkie. From time to time, there are closeups of his hands maneuvering over the keys and, if you can overcome the fascination of the ring, you can discover how cleverly those fingers dash across the eighty-eight. He decorates the tune with arpeggios, trills, and other high-handed gimmicks. When he uses a dramatic two-handed chord, he has the habit of bringing his hands up over his head. The number ends.

Liberace rises from his piano bench and approaches you. He speaks softly, almost suggestively. He thanks a little old lady from New England for sending him a homemade quilt. He recalls how he was privileged to play at a Veterans Administration hospital, and how "the boys" enjoyed his visit, but especially how much he enjoyed visiting them, "the poor souls."

When this is over, there is a change of pace. Liberace is happy again. "My brother George plays a really hot fiddle," he says as brother George trots out with a few sidemen to play his violin.

"Time to go," Liberace says sadly. "Wish we had more time for your requests." He plays "I'll Be Seeing You" and he is suddenly lit in silhouette again, just him, his piano, and his candelabra. And then he is gone.

The abominable showman.

LETTERS TO LIBERACE

These are excerpts from Liberace's fan mail received during the 1950s:

"We are all greatly touched by the genuine humility of your voice. I am well aware how such a voice can soothe the sick and suffering."

"I love your smile, dimple and mischievous wink (like a little boy's). I know you have a wonderful mother for you're a wonderful man."

"I think it is wonderful that you are not at all temperamental. With all your success, you are so patient and seem to have time to be nice to all us fans."

"For many years, my mother has admired you and I mean admired you! She enjoys you so much that sometimes she makes Dad mad. . . . Sometimes, Mom says she would just love a piece of your shirt or an old sock, but I know that is too much to ask."

"When you're married to a grouch, a man who never smiles or says thank you for anything, you look forward to Liberace just to see him smile."

"I want you to meet my brother George," Liberace used to say. It became an oft-quoted expression of the 1950s, much like "you bet your bippy" belonged to the 1960s.

In Chicago in the early 1950s, columnist Claudia Cassidy wrote a particularly scathing attack on Liberace. The following evening, Lee read the review to his concert audience, adding: "Thank you for your very amusing review. After reading it, in fact, my brother George and I laughed all the way to the bank." And that's where that expression got started.

"I think the people who like me most have found their lives lacking in some way," Liberace said, trying to explain his mass appeal. "Maybe they have routine jobs and find relief in me and my career. Some don't have money and my programs give them something glamorous." Here, Lee pauses for a sip of coffee, from a paper cup.

Before lucking out with a local Los Angeles TV show, Liberace and his brother George were earning $500 a week as a concert attraction. Three years later, his TV show was on 190 stations and the Riviera Hotel in Las Vegas booked him for $50,000 a week. Ah, the power of the tube.

SOME KIND WORDS FROM...

William Connor of the *London Daily Mirror:*
"The biggest sentimental vomit of all time!"

Irving Sablosky of the *Chicago News:*
"I wanted to cry help!"

The *Norfolk Virginian-Pilot:*
"In the ascendancy of Liberace's star to its current zenith we are witnessing another triumph of mediocrity."

Faye Emerson of the *New York World-Telegram:*
"Such dimpling and winking! Such tossing of blond curls, and fluttering of eyelashes and flashing of teeth! Such nausea!"

When he started out in the business, Liberace, whose real name is Wladziu Valentino Liberace, used the name Buster Keys.

THE BUSINESS BEHIND THE BOX

A blue light bounced off the shiny teeth of a pianist as he played "Stardust" in a packed Ciro's nightclub in Hollywood. Don Fedderson, then head of L.A.'s Channel 13, waited for the number to finish, then stopped by to ask Liberace, the pianist, to come to his office the next day to talk about a television show. "Wonderful!" exclaimed the Milwaukee-born musician. "I'll be there early."

At 9 A.M., Liberace pranced into Fedderson's office, carrying two huge cookbooks. Curious, Fedderson asked him about the hefty tomes. "Well," Liberace began, "I want to tell you how my show will go." He then proceeded to explain to the broadcaster that he wanted to do a cooking show, not a piano program. Fedderson regained his equilibrium, then patiently explained he wasn't interested in cooking; he wanted Lee to play the piano. Later, against the advice of his friends and associates, Fedderson signed Liberace to headline a weekly fifteen-minute show which debuted in the spring of 1951.

Seymour Heller, Liberace's long-time personal manager, recalls: "Lee was always a good act. He had a certain magnetism that got over to nightclub people. He could hold them for an hour and a half. Fedderson told me that if we could capture that same quality on television, we'd have 'lightning in a bottle.' As it turns out, Lee's basic magnetism was magnified by TV. He looked right into the camera, made you feel that he was performing just for you. Why, we knew of women who came to believe that he was in *love* with them because his approach was so direct and personal."

Before Liberace's first TV outing was over, the station's (then KLAC, not KCOP) switchboard was ablaze. The Citizen's Trust and Savings Bank picked up sponsorship and soon became the merriest money merchant in Los Angeles. The bank offered a free Liberace record album for every ten-dollar account opened, and within three months, the financial institution had taken in $600,000. Liberace was an overnight sensation.

"I knew that once I got the chance to look into that camera real hard," Liberace recalls, "the country would know me for a friend."

He got his first taste of network exposure as Dinah Shore's 1952 summer replacement when he had the chance to appear twice weekly for fifteen minutes on NBC. The run was only thirteen weeks in duration, but it was a turning point. Guild Films Company, Inc., a principal purveyor of canned TV programs, decided to take a flyer with Liberace by producing a new half-hour version of *The Liberace Show* and distributing it on a syndicated basis to stations all around the country. The first such sale was made in the spring of 1953 to station KBTV in Denver. Although the show caught on immediately with the public, it was still hard to sell in new territory. Finally it began to snowball, reaching at its peak more than 200 stations every week.

"We had 217 different sponsors at one time," recalls Liberace. "There were thirty-eight banks, two funeral homes, bakeries, even an underwear manufacturer."

The 117 half-hour films, shot at a cost of $10,000 each at the Beverly Hills Theatre, had a viewership of some 30 million people. Its star had won two Emmys, for Best Entertainment Program of 1952 and as Outstanding Male Personality. He was TV's first genuine matinee idol. The program was being telecast throughout the United States, Hawaii, Alaska, Canada, Cuba, and Venezuela. It was estimated that his appearances had brought some $50 million worth of new business to his sponsors in just one year! *TV Guide* called him "something of an Eighth Wonder of the Show Business World." His mail was reaching 10,000 pieces a week, mostly from middle-aged women, who made up the bulk of his syndicated audience.

Liberace fans were a die-hard lot. After Omaha and Cleveland TV stations started carrying the program, TV repairmen in these cities reported an unusual breakage of picture tubes. "On a few sets I found lipstick on the busted glass," said one mechanic.

After two years, Liberace decided to call it quits. He felt he was overexposing himself on TV. "I'm purposely staying off TV," he said at the time. "I feel a demand for me must be re-created, and to re-create it I must be missed." For years, Liberace's TV films were being shown in countless U.S. cities. Viewers in Washington, D. C., for instance, could tune him in five times a week in 1958 on WTTG. The shows were in their twelfth rerun.

"In the old days all I had to do was walk out on the stage and the audience was in my hand," Lee said. "Now people have a 'show me' attitude. I have to work like the devil to convince them I'm good."

What a lot of work for one man.

ME AND THE CHIMP

THE GUILTY PARTIES

Creator/Executive Producer:	Garry K. Marshall
Producer:	Alan Rafkin
Directors:	Oscar Rudolph, Roger Duchowny, Alan Rafkin, Richard Kinon, Garry K. Marshall, Ted Bessell
Writers:	Garry K. Marshall, Gordon Farr, Arnold Kane, Joseph and Betty Bonaduce, Mickey Rose, Bob Rogers, Larry Markes, Frank Buxton, Ron Friedman
Cameraman:	Leonard South
Film Editors:	Jerry Dronsky, Bob Phillips
Music by:	Charles Fox

A Paramount Television production for CBS-TV.

Starring Ted Bessell as Mike Reynolds, Anita Gillette as Liz Reynolds, Scott Kolden as Scott Reynolds, Kami Cotler as Kitty Reynolds, and Jackie the chimp as Buttons the chimp.

Debuted Thursday, January 13, 1972, 8 P.M. E.S.T. on CBS-TV.

THE FORMAT

"In *Me and the Chimp,* I thought of Cary Grant in *Bringing Up Baby,*" remarked *Chimp* leading man, Ted Bessell. What Bessell failed to realize was that he is not Cary Grant and *Me and the Chimp* is not in any way like that wonderful 1938 screwball comedy about a family and their pet leopard.

Young Scott Reynolds (Scott Kolden) and his little sister Kitty (Kami Cotler) are playing around a drainpipe near their home in San Pascal, California, when they discover a playful little chimpanzee. They take the scared little scamp, who has escaped from an Air Force research center, home to meet their parents, Liz (Anita Gillette) and Mike Reynolds (Ted Bessell), a dentist.

The children want to adopt the creature immediately, but Daddy is not easily won over. He makes an agreement with his wife that if he spends an entire day with the monkey and still doesn't warm up to him, they won't keep him. First Mike tries to balance his checkbook on an adding machine with the chimp staring at him. "Do you have to look at me that way?" the dentist asks (the laugh track went absolutely ape . . . er, wild over that one), before getting up to answer the door. When he returns to his paperwork, his balance is off by about $23,000. "How," he asks himself, "could I push so many wrong buttons?" He does a take. "Buttons! That's it," and so the chimp is named.

The following day, a Saturday, Mike decides to go into the office to take care of an emergency patient, a grande dame type (Reta Shaw). Buttons goes along for a visit. Naturally, all the comedy stops are pulled out on this scene with Buttons taking over the tooth extraction. They should have used laughing gas to put all of us to sleep. And this was one of the funnier spots.

In another episode, Mike is locked out of his house and gets Buttons to climb up a tree, get in the window and get his keys. "You're more fun than a barrel of people," Mike permits, congratulating the chimp on his feat. But now Buttons has learned to steal and in no time, he's turned into a regular klepto.

The thirteen episodes, ranging from poor to downright awful, represented the dreariest potboilers ever dished up by a network, particularly the kinglike CBS who had just blazed trails with *All in the Family*. A network vice president, in charge of new projects, admits that CBS was so eager to make a long-term contract with Bessell, that they actually opted for a series everyone knew *in front* would croak.

Well, it's nice to be in Bessell's shoes, certainly, but what about the networks' responsibility to those of us who lend them the use of *our* airwaves?

MEMORABLE MOMENTS

- "The Lost Flashlight"—Buttons loses his flashlight and the neighborhood is in a turmoil while it's missing.
- "Mike's Burglar Alarm"—Mike teaches Buttons about a burglar alarm, but winds up on a police lineup.
- "Buttons and Juliet"—Buttons falls in love with Mildred, another chimpanzee.
- "Tennis, Anyone?"—Buttons dons tennis whites to teach some country club snobs a lesson in bigotry.

After five years with Marlo Thomas, Ted Bessell tried his luck with a chimpanzee. "Everybody tells me that if the show's a hit, it's because of the monkey," said Bessell shortly before the premiere of *Me and the Chimp* in 1972. "If it flops, it's my fault."

"I don't care for the monkey," Bessell snorted on the set. "This has got to be the giant mistake of my life!" The chimp was Jackie, three and a half years old, owned by Lou Schumacher.

Anita Gillette played Liz Reynolds on *Me and the Chimp*. She distinguished herself on the Broadway stage with starring roles in *Cabaret* and Woody Allen's *Don't Drink the Water*. A year later, she costarred in the TV version of *Bob & Carol & Ted & Alice* which ran fewer weeks than *Chimp*.

Chimp Jackie, who played chimp Buttons on *Me and the Chimp*, was, according to her trainer Bob Riedell, "unpredictable, strong and potentially dangerous." (A chimpanzee once bit Ray Walston working in a *My Favorite Martian* episode, requiring considerable hospital treatment.) Her salary was $1,000 per week, or approximately two tons of bananas.

The cast of *Me and the Chimp*, including the youngsters Kami Cotler (who went on to play Elizabeth on *The Waltons*, the show that took over the *Chimp* time slot) and Scott Kolden. Bessell looks uneasy. "I used to pet dogs at a distance. I'm tired of all the puddles on the set— I've ruined three pairs of shoes already," Bessell said after shooting seven of the thirteen *Chimp* shows.

SOME KIND WORDS FROM ...

Harlan Ellison of the *Los Angeles Free Press:*
"A witless farrago of clichés and creaking sitcom banalities. . . ."

Fred Silverman, programing executive:
"Represents a new depth in TV programing."

Cleveland Amory of *TV Guide:*
"This is a show on two levels—ours and the chimp's. On the chimp's level, it's terrific."

THE BUSINESS BEHIND THE BOX

In early 1953—at about the time Little Ricky was born on *I Love Lucy*—a ten-month-old chimpanzee with the curious name J. Fred Muggs, made his debut on NBC's *Today Show*. Within a month of his appearance, the ratings of the early morning show had improved dramatically. Dick Pinkham, *Today's* early executive producer, claims: "That wretched little ape did more to put the show over the top than our news coverage."

That "ape," today an attraction at Busch Gardens in Tampa, Florida, was responsible for initiating the strange love affair between monkeys and the medium of television. *Super Circus, Daktari, Jungle Jim,* and *The Hathaways* (a 1961 sitcom starring Peggy Cass and Jack Weston as "parents" of a trio of chimps) are just a sampling of shows with a simian point of view.

On January 13, 1972 (it was *not* a Friday), CBS aired for the first time *Me and the Chimp,* promoting it "creatively," with "There's more fun than a barrel of monkeys when a dentist's family adopts a chimp who refuses to mind his own monkey business!" This was the show CBS, then the Number One network, chose to replace *Bearcats,* an adventure starring Rod Taylor and Dennis Cole. Why in the world, you ask? Let's try to figure it out.

Actor Ted Bessell was riding high on the wave of success generated by his costarring role with Marlo Thomas in *That Girl,* a sitcom that went off ABC after a healthy five-year run in 1971. One of the hottest stars in town, he made a pilot for Bill Persky, his *That Girl* producer, about a guy in analysis but NBC, who bankrolled it, was scared of the subject matter. It was, by all indications, ahead of its time. Bessell had firm offers for six other series when Garry Marshall, producer of *The Odd Couple,* came to him with an idea titled *The Chimp and I.*

Marshall, today "godfather" to *Happy Days, Laverne and Shirley,* and *Mork and Mindy,* had begun his comedy-writing career as a contributor of gags to Jack Paar, then had become a full-fledged writer for Joey Bishop before teaming up with Jerry Belson to produce scripts for Lucille Ball, *The Dick Van Dyke Show,* and others.

"Tom Miller wanted to do a show about a chimp," Marshall recalls about a conversation he had with the Paramount production executive. "At the time I was looking for a show that kids would like, and adults, too." Marshall, a W. C. Fields aficionado, thought a comedy with a monkey offered possibilities for Fieldsian humor. "On TV," he explains, "you can't do a show about a man who doesn't like babies (the Fields staple), but you *can* do a show about a man who doesn't like chimps. So that's how I wrote the pilot."

For $50,000, Marshall and Miller put together a sixteen-minute "presentation" film. Alan Wagner, a CBS West Coast program executive, saw the sample and liked it. Fred Silverman, then head of the CBS network, was shown the film by Tom Tannenbaum, head of production for Paramount.

"Silverman felt it was the kind of programing that had a chance against Flip," Tannenbaum recounts. (Flip Wilson's variety show was the second most popular show in the nation, after *All in the Family*.)

Silverman's choice (he assured CBS affiliates that the show was going to "make the whole country chimp-conscious") was a ratings disaster from day one. It opened with a 16 Nielsen rating to Flip Wilson's 28 and *Alias Smith and Jones's* 17. The numbers never improved, and neither did the climate on the Paramount set of *Chimp*.

Star Bessell, who was earning $7,500 a week, took an immediate dislike to the chimp Jackie. "For six million years the monkeys of the world have been working up to this show. I've stayed my distance from her all through the filming. Nobody sees the looks she gives me—the times when she shows her teeth. If we can get canceled in thirteen weeks, my life may be saved."

Bessell's wish was granted. The show was canceled (replaced that fall by *The Waltons*) and aired for the last time on May 18, 1972, with a Nielsen rating of 9.

"We had concept problems," Paramount's Tannenbaum complained. "Bessell saw it one way, we saw it another. He felt he should always be against the chimp staying in his house, while everybody else wanted the chimp to stay."

Garry Marshall claims: "The dentist didn't like the chimp, but they played it that the chimp got into trouble and he got it out. That appealed to the kids, but the adult element was gone."

One corporate executive at Paramount grumbled, "We cast the wrong chimp."

MICKEY

THE GUILTY PARTIES

Executive Producer:	Selig J. Seligman
Producers/Writers:	Robert Fisher, Arthur Marx
Director:	Richard Whorf
Cameraman:	Fleetwood Southcott
Film Editor:	Floyd Knudtson
Casting:	Marvin Paige

A Selmur Production in association with MGM Television for ABC-TV.

Starring Mickey Rooney as Mickey Grady, Emmaline Henry as Nora Grady, Sammee Tong as Sammy Ling, Timmy Rooney as Timmy Grady, Brian Nash as Buddy Grady, and Bobby Van as Bobby.

Debuted Wednesday, September 16, 1964, 9 P.M. E.D.T. on ABC-TV.

THE FORMAT

Mickey Grady (Mickey Rooney) inherits a motel at Newport Beach, California, a modest little seaside resort, variously called the Marine Palms Motel, the Newport Arms, and the Newport Palms, leaving the relative calm of his hometown of Omaha for the rigors of Southern California.

With his patient wife Nora (Emmaline Henry) and sons Timmy (Timmy Rooney, son of the star), and Buddy (Brian Nash), Mickey arrives at the probated hostelry only to find one Sammy Ling (Sammee Tong) who promptly announces that he has a lifetime contract and cannot be fired. Mickey asks to see the books. "You're looking at them," announces the lippy Ling stoically. "You don't keep books??" Mickey inquires incredulously. "This way much better . . . in case of fire, books can jump out window." And so the jokes go.

The hotel is so deeply in the red because Sammy has been cutting his various relatives in on the pie. For instance, Sammy's lawyer cousin, "Loophole" Ling, does all the hotel legal work while a Ling Savings and Loan holds the mortgage . . . at 17½ percent annual interest.

The situations are about as promising as the dialogue ("Only registered guests are permitted to drown in the pool," etc.). In one tiresome episode with Dina Merrill playing a wealthy femme fatale Mickey is trapped on her yacht, and has a helluva time keeping away from her. He ends up, fully clothed, in the drink, and when he does finally escape, it's in her mink coat and nothing else. When he arrives back at his hotel, he has to ask manager Ling for money to pay the taxi driver. Says Ling: "Old Chinese saying, 'Never lend money to man in mink.' "

We know another ancient Oriental proverb: "Never put sinking ships in water."

MEMORABLE MOMENTS

- Mickey's freeloading brother-in-law Bobby arrives in a trunk marked C.O.D.
- Mickey thinks his eyes are playing tricks on him—he's just seen a water-skiing elephant.
- Mickey takes Buddy and some fellow Cub Scouts on an overnight camping trip.

Mickey-Times-Three: Mickey Rooney donned many disguises to play his role of Mickey Grady. They weren't enough—we still recognized him as the perpetrator of this sorry sitcom.

"Our show has good humor," said Mickey Rooney weeks before his sitcom premiered on ABC in 1964. "It's in good taste and it's elastic. Things don't happen to Mickey; Mickey happens to things." Like *Mickey* happened to get canceled.

Sammee Tong endeared himself to millions of TV viewers as the wisecracking Peter on *Bachelor Father*, the long-running sitcom starring John Forsythe. He accepted the supporting role on *Mickey* after a two-year hiatus from series television. He took his life shortly before the show got canned.

Sandwiched between regular roles on *I'm Dickens, He's Fenster* and *I Dream of Jeannie*, Emmaline Henry portrayed Mickey Rooney's wife Nora for seventeen weeks in the actor's ill-fated 1964 sitcom.

THE BUSINESS BEHIND THE BOX

During MGM's heyday—the 1930s and 1940s—Mickey Rooney was responsible for bringing in more business to neighborhood movie houses than just about anybody, except Shirley Temple. His *Andy Hardy* films made millions for the Metro-Goldwyn-Mayer moguls; young Rooney could do no wrong.

Then television rolled around, and in 1954 Mickey, now thirty-two years of age, got his first crack at it when NBC offered up *Hey, Mulligan*, a sitcom *TV Guide* called "a shambles." The show miraculously lasted thirty-nine weeks but just about killed Mickey's chances for a small screen career. Then, ten years later, ABC granted the entertainer his second chance. Under the production aegis of Selmur Productions, the comedy-writing team of Bob Fisher and Arthur Marx (Groucho's son) put together a show called *Mickey*.

"I felt a little self-conscious about calling it *Mickey*," explained Rooney. "I thought it was a little egotistical. But we couldn't very well call it *Irving*. And, after all, I figure I've been in this business forty-two years: I deserve a little stroking." The producers assembled a cast consisting almost entirely of seasoned TV series alumni. To play Mickey's wife they brought in Emmaline Henry, fresh out of *I'm Dickens, He's Fenster.* To play one of Rooney's two sons, Timmy Rooney was given the nepotistic nod. He had had experience playing a juvenile in the short-lived sitcom *Room for One More.* To play the Chinese hotel manager, Sammee Tong, a veteran of five years on *Bachelor Father,* was hired. With a group as experienced as this, how could *Mickey* fail?

Well, first off, ABC plopped it into one of the most impossible time slots of the season—opposite CBS's powerhouse Emmy-winner, *The Dick Van Dyke Show,* and the opening half-hour of NBC's high-budget Wednesday night movie. The network tried the old ploy of starting two weeks sooner than the competition, but that hardly made an ounce of difference. *Mickey* was in trouble even before it left the starting gate.

By mid-November, 1964, *Mickey* had run out of steam, and ABC pink-slipped the sitcom, agreeing to air the seventeen episodes already filmed. It was a big blow to Rooney who needed the money to support his ex-wives and children. The network turned over the time period to *Shindig,* a burgeoning rock show.

When the ax fell, a cloud of doom hung over the entire *Mickey* company when it was learned that Sammee Tong had committed suicide at his Los Angeles home. The sixty-three-year-old actor, who had played the part of Sammy Ling on the series, took his own life just a week or so before the cancellation.

Rooney himself blamed the show's demise on the Van Dyke show. "It's a superior show. I knew what we were up against when we went in. You know, you just can't take the public for granted anymore."

MISS AMERICA PAGEANTS

THE GUILTY PARTIES

Executive Producer:	Albert A. Marks, Jr.
Producers:	John Koushouris,
	George Cavalier
Director:	Tim Kiley
Writer:	Angela Osborne
Associate Producer:	Nanci Linke-Ellis
Choreographer:	Ron Poindexter
Musical Director:	Glenn Osser

A Miss America Pageants production in association with NBC-TV.
Starring Bob Russell (1954) and Bert Parks (1955–present) as hosts.
Debuted Saturday, September 11, 1954, 10:30 P.M. E.D.T. on ABC-TV.

THE FORMAT

While spotlights crisscross the more than 25,000 people crammed into the cavernous old Convention Hall, a voice heralds "live from Atlantic City"—and yet *another* Miss America Pageant begins. Like the annual December screenings of *Miracle on 34th Street* and the New Year's Day telecast of the Rose Bowl events, the second week of September is reserved for Bert Parks and the *Miss America Pageant*.

The show begins as it does every year with the state representatives pouring out of the wings, pausing briefly for an announcer to relay the girl's name and home state. These ladies represent the efforts of over 3,500 local pageants where some 70,000 contestants have been considered. Each state winner began competing on a hometown level, working her way up to the state contest and then on to Atlantic City. The local pageants usually are sponsored by the Jaycees, a predominantly white middle-class civic group. This may be part of the reason why each year the winners tend to look like the winners from past years: WASP clones in one-piece bathing suits.

What millions of international viewers see on that fateful September evening is merely the last leg of a week-long treadmill of interviews and modeling by the girls. Nine judges not only have watched each contestant display her talent and poise, but also have seen her in a bathing suit and evening gown. The judges award up to five points for bathing suit and evening gown categories and up to ten points for the talent display. All of this before the telecast Saturday night.

The ten girls with the most points get to perform their talents on TV (we are told that it is more important to have a pretty and charming Miss America than a talented one). Sometimes these talents—and we use the word advisedly—seem better suited to another television show, of the *Gong* variety.

At some point in the proceedings, each of the ten finalists chats with Parks. Prior to 1972, one question was asked of each girl, but this method was discarded because, as one pageant official noted, "The questions too often were written—and answered—inanely."

The judges give their final decisions to a trusty CPA who scurries offstage, tallies the votes, and then turns over his findings to Parks. The modern day ritual concludes when Parks takes a dramatic deep breath and announces the names of the fourth, third, second, and first runners-up. This leaves but one girl—statistically, she will be nineteen years old, 5'6" tall, weigh 123 pounds, have blue eyes, brown hair, and a 34-24-35 figure—who immediately buries her face in her manicured hands. With a countenance contorted with happiness, she assists Parks with the rhinestone crown, grabs the fresh roses, and, as Bert begins The Song, she starts her way down the runway and into the hearts of millions who will not even remember her name over breakfast the following morning.

MEMORABLE MOMENTS

- When Miss Montana rode her palomino onstage, the horse fell into the orchestra pit.

- A finalist did an impression of Ed Sullivan.

- Miss Nebraska of 1962 accidentally threw a flaming baton into the judges' box.

- One "talent" demonstration was an archer shooting balloons out of her father's hand.

- The doves in Miss Idaho's act got loose and flew all over the Hall.

- Once Bert Parks was given the wrong list of girls' names, then muttered: "Somebody screwed this up good!"

- And who could forget Miss Nebraska's impression of a beatnik?

SOME KIND WORDS FROM ...

John Canaday of the *New York Times:*
"[Miss America] is no longer a real creature formed, like the rest of us, by normal processes of biological growth and social conditioning, but has become only a girl-like product synthesized from fleshlike plastic and marketed with slight annual changes in the packaging ..."

Saturday Review:
"... [Miss Americas] all resemble Anne Rutherford in an old Andy Hardy movie."

Shana Alexander of *Life* magazine:
"[The Pageant] is dull and pretentious and racist and exploitative and icky and sad. It is fake in everything from wigs to talents to sentiments. It does not worship beauty but beauty products. Though the girls are not fakes, they themselves are treated as products. Beauty contests are not so much antifemale as they are antihuman. The complication of the so-called "talent contest" obliges them to conspire in their own humiliation. And despite all the schmaltz and sanitizing, there clings to the proceedings a strong taint of the auction block."

Bert Parks poses in his rented finery as he anticipates yet another edition of the *Miss America Pageant.* He's as much a part of the institution as the girls themselves.

"Bertie," the boys on the boardwalk in Atlantic City call him. Once one of TV's busiest emcees—hosting as many as a dozen shows a week—Parks now can afford to work only one night a year. His take is somewhere in the neighborhood of $35,000. Nice neighborhood.

Maria Beale Fletcher, Miss America 1962. This Miss North Carolina was nineteen years of age, boasted a 35-24-35 figure and stood five feet, five and one-half inches tall. Shana Alexander once called Miss Americas, "living Barbie dolls with styrofoam smiles."

Answering to a higher authority or interviewing a rather tall Miss America, Bert Parks began the hosting chores in 1955. Johnny Carson once quipped: "Talking to Miss America is like talking to a redwood tree." So much for the National Forests.

Bert Parks flanked by two Miss Americas—Donna Axum, 1964, and Bess Myerson, 1945. They don't make 'em the way they used to.

The Pageant format is not the only thing that shows its age. Here, Bert Parks poses for the Fifty-fourth Annual Pageant telecast in 1974, his twentieth anniversary as host.

FROM THE HORSE'S . . . (Bert Parks)

Q: How do the negative things said about the *Pageant* affect you?

A: None of the criticism bothers me. I've been criticized by the best. In the case of *Miss America,* I know that I'm generally seen in a very sympathetic light. It is a high prestige position and damned good exposure.

Q: Has your career suffered any because of the strong identification with the *Pageant* you enjoy?

A: I think it *may* have hurt my career *in* television. But I like the *Pageant,* and I think I do a damned good job at what I'm supposed to do. I'm a catalyst, and I never forget that it is not my show. It is the girls' show. I work for them.

Q: What do *you* think is the appeal of the *Pageant?*

A: It's the old American dream, the old frustration of wanting "royalty" and never having it. In all the years I've been doing this show, it's never failed that when Miss America walks down that runway, the audience rises to its feet. I've never seen so much adulation given to anyone other than the Queen of England.

Q: What do you think of the feminists who regularly attack the *Pageant?*

A: I think most of them are disgruntled young ladies. A psychiatrist would have a ball with them. I have grave doubts about their sexuality. All I know is one of them used to play left end for Notre Dame! That's not exactly our idea of a feminine woman. If you've ever looked at them, there's not much chance of their ever becoming a real human being.

NOTE: On December 30, 1979, while celebrating his sixty-fifth birthday, Bert Parks received word from an Associated Press reporter that he had been fired as emcee of the *Pageant*—"retired," the official report claimed. The Pageant's headquarters in Atlantic City were inundated with phone calls, all of them mourning Parks' "passing." Johnny Carson urged his *Tonight* show viewers to "mail postcards" to New Jersey; bumper stickers, screaming SAVE BERT PARKS, were immediately fashioned; and one newspaper reporter wrote, "I'm not watching it, no matter if they get Luciano Pavarotti to sing 'There She Is' . . ." The official word from the Pageant promoters; "We're trying to be modern, contemporary, . . . to play to a youthful audience, . . . to hype up the show and 'be with it,' as the kids say." Such names as Mac Davis and John Davidson were being considered as Parks' replacement at the time of this writing. Davis said, "I wouldn't touch the job with a ten-foot pole."

THE BUSINESS BEHIND THE BOX

The *Miss America Pageant* had been quietly crowning beauty queens of that lofty title since 1921 (excusing itself for six Depression years), but not until September 11, 1954, did the event burst forth in all its questionable glory on nationwide television courtesy of the ABC Network.

That Saturday night more than 27 million girl-watchers saw nineteen-year-old Lee Meriwether, "Miss California," being crowned by pageant host Bob Russell (Bert Parks didn't take over the chores until the following year). Meriwether's dad had died just a few weeks before the occasion and when Lee stepped forward to accept the crown from Miss America 1954, Evelyn Ay, she turned her eyes toward heaven and said, "You know I know how happy you are," then let loose a flood of tears that lasted until the last Philco commercial faded out. That manufacturer had paid a meager $10,000 for the privilege of sponsoring the first pageant, an exercise in middle-class ethics. Some 39 percent of all available TV viewers that night tuned in, beating out *Your Hit Parade* and a game show, *Two for the Money*. (For the same "privilege" in 1955, Philco forked over $25,000, but the affair garnered a whopping 41 percent audience share this time out.)

The year 1955 also marked the beginning of the pageant as we know it today. Bert Parks, an emcee who had made a minor name for himself as a radio game show host (*Stop the Music, Double Or Nothing*) and a TV quizmaster (*Break the Bank*), accepted the pageant director's invitation to Atlantic City, perennial site of the annual affair, to host the event. It was also the year in which the song "There She Is, Miss America" was heard. Written by Bernie Wayne and introduced on a *Philco Playhouse* drama about what happens to a Miss America after her reign, the tune is so closely associated with the pageant now that in 1968, when an attempt was made to upgrade the tenor of the televised proceedings by dropping the tune, protests by the thousands poured in and the decision was reversed.

In 1957 CBS lured the pageant away from ABC, and the ratings soared (over half of the available audience watched) so phenomenally that the 1958 pageant was expanded to ninety minutes. The move paid off in an even larger viewing audience (two-thirds of all TV homes tuned in). This meant that in less than five years, the pageant ratings had doubled; more than 60 million folks were ogling the beauties. With every passing Labor Day, the numbers rose (the show went to NBC in 1966) until they peaked in 1970, when it was estimated that over 80 million Americans were right there in the Convention Hall alongside the 25,000 paid admissions.

Who are these *Miss America Pageant* aficionados? We're told that the annual rite appeals to females between the ages of twelve and seventy-five. What began as an exhibition for leering men on the Atlantic City boardwalk had become a case of women checking out the "competition."

Time has passed Miss America by. She is a relic—albeit a wholesome artifact—of what America was supposed to expect of its young women. Even Pepsi Cola, one of the show's major sponsors until 1968, pulled out of the pageant because "Miss America was totally out of touch with kids and the cities." The soft drink spokesman also offered: "Miss America as run today does not represent the changing values of our society."

Not so coincidentally, pageant officials began attempts to contemporize the show. Until 1969, contestants were required to wear three-inch spike heels and a one-piece bathing suit (which, in the days when bikinis were the only popular swimsuit style, sometimes posed a problem for those contestants who had to purchase these "costumes"). The evening gowns had to be within two inches of the knee at a time when mini-skirts were all the rage. Miss New York of 1969 recalls: "The problem was that we couldn't *find* dresses that were long enough so that when we let them down they would be long enough."

To this day, few shows outdraw *Miss America* in the ratings race. The Super Bowl, the Academy Awards presentation, and a few Bob Hope specials earn equally high numbers, prompting one network executive to ponder: "Were Bob Hope to crown Miss America at halftime of the Super Bowl, the nation would crunch to a complete halt, since figures prove conclusively that every man, woman and child in the United States would be watching television at that moment."

MY LIVING DOLL

THE GUILTY PARTIES

Creators:	Al Martin and Bill Kelsay from an idea by Leo Guild
Executive Producer:	Jack Chertok
Producer:	Howard Leeds
Production Executive:	Harry Poppe
Directors:	Lawrence Dobkin, Ezra Stone, et al.
Writers:	Al Martin, Bill Kelsay, et al.
Cameraman:	Glenn MacWilliams
Film Editors:	Jodi Copelan, Ted Rich
Music by:	George Greeley
Casting:	Lynn Stalmaster

A Jack Chertok TV production in association with the CBS Television Network for CBS-TV.

Starring Robert Cummings as Dr. Robert McDonald, Julie Newmar as Rhoda Miller, Jack Mullaney as Peter Robinson, Doris Dowling as Irene Adams, and Henry Beckman as Carl Miller.

Debuted Sunday, September 27, 1964, 9 P.M. E.D.T. on CBS-TV.

THE FORMAT

"Here is a woman, very intelligent. A perfect mind, a perfect body, but no emotions," Julie Newmar once said, describing her role as Rhoda the robot on CBS's *My Living Doll* series. "She does not nag, she does not complain. She is never contentious. She is utterly guileless. It is the psychiatrist who must invest her with personality. Bob, who is the doctor, is the symbol of the strong male image.

She'll do anything he programs for her, anything he commands. He must even teach her to love."

Lucky Bob. Can you imagine how many viewers sat out there in TV-land on Sunday nights with their tongues hanging out, ready and willing to sell their souls to trade shoes with Julie's costar Bob Cummings? To be in command of a female robot, one who looks like Miss Newmar ... well, it's just too much to imagine.

Dr. Robert McDonald (Robert Cummings) is an Air Force base psychiatrist who is assigned by his friend Dr. Carl Miller (Henry Beckman), an aerospace scientist, to take over his latest creation, Air Force Project 709. Rhoda, as the project is later nicknamed, just happens to be a perfect woman. Well, not quite a woman. She's a robot. Oh, not your run-of-the-mill robot with metal armor and dials. Rhoda's six feet tall, has huge breasts (she needs 'em—that's where her solar batteries are stored!), shapely thighs, and a face like a movie star. Why not? Rhoda's played by Julie Newmar who is six feet tall, has huge ... you get the idea.

It just so happens that one day Rhoda wanders into Doc McDonald's office at the base. They hit it off quite well—the shrink is a lecherous bachelor boy—and when the robot's creator, Dr. Miller, is called away for reassignment, Rhoda is left in the care of McDonald, who promises to mold her character, along the lines of what Professor Higgins did with Eliza Doolittle.

Bob lives with his sister Irene (Doris Dowling) who raises more than her eyebrow when Bob brings Rhoda home. He tells his sister that she is a patient of his, one who requires constant attention. Because of the Air Force secrecy requirement, the truth about AF 709 cannot be revealed. No sooner has Rhoda arrived when the swinging playboy next door, Peter Robinson (Jack Mullaney), drops by to introduce himself. He is immediately struck by one of Cupid's most powerful arrows, and now McDonald's duty is doubly difficult: He has to keep the lecherous Robinson from making advances, lest he discover for himself that her beauty really *is* only skin deep.

Occasionally, McDonald must adjust Rhoda's circuitry and does so by fiddling with the four cleverly disguised dials on her upper back (everyone thinks they're just beauty marks). But training her to be the "perfect" woman—whatever *that* is—is McDonald's main task. That is until Cummings quit the show before it ran its course, and Rhoda had to shack up with Robinson next door.

The situations were pat and predictable. How many times were we to be subjected to the conflict of Rhoda's perfection and the imperfection, or humanness, of those around her? Talk about a one-joke show (and a bad joke at that). This one deserved the *My Mother, the Car* award for ludicrousness.

MEMORABLE MOMENTS

■ Bob's escorting a General's daughter to a reception for a VIP and he gives strict orders that Rhoda's not to leave the apartment.

- Bob gets off to an inauspicious start as chairman of a road-safety committee: He rams into his neighbor's car.

- Reading *Alice in Wonderland* has had a peculiar effect on poor Rhoda: She's afflicted with spells of dizziness.

- Bob's friend Herb would rather be a comic than a pharmacist, but Bob's been asked to persuade the young man to stick to filling prescriptions.

Curvaceous Julie Newmar, age twenty-nine, and loquacious Robert Cummings, age fifty-four, stars of CBS's ill-fated *My Living Doll*. From the moment this pair stepped onto the Desilu soundstage, they began a running feud that culminated in Cummings's resignation. "Fifteen steps, turn and fire!"

Air Force Project 709, better known as Rhoda the robot, gets an arm wrenching from Dr. Bob McDonald, a psychiatrist whose job it is to make her the "perfect" woman.

© J. Ryan

SOME KIND WORDS FROM ...

Frank Judge of the *Detroit News*:
"Once you've seen one robot show, you've seen them all...."

TV Guide:
"... infantile."

Anthony LaCamera of the *Boston Record American*:
"One long, tiresome, leering joke."

Bob Cummings, Jack Mullaney, and Julie Newmar rehearse a scene from "Pool Shark," one of the twenty-six *My Living Doll* episodes. Critics were *not* carried away by this series.

Julie Newmar: "Once in a while I will sidle up to a mirror and plant a kiss on it and squeal something about how beautiful I am."

When Cummings stormed off the set in a huff, actor Jack Mullaney became the robot's Svengali. Mullaney had already appeared in two series, *The Ann Sothern Show* and *Ensign O'Toole.*

THE BUSINESS BEHIND THE BOX

Among Jim Aubrey's legion of show business friends was one Julie Newmar, an actress of considerable proportions, once described by columnist Sidney Skolsky as "a great construction job." Aubrey, the CBS television chieftain of the early 1960s, was bent on finding the right vehicle for the young star who had won a Tony Award for her 1959 performance in Broadway's *Marriage-Go-Round*, with Charles Boyer. Aubrey felt, and rightly so, that she was a "natural" for the tube. She qualified for CBS, according to Aubrey's dictum: "Sexy dolls, no old people . . . and no physical infirmities." His code was unwritten but quite rigid.

Jack Chertok, a seasoned TV producer, happened to hear about Aubrey's plans for Newmar through the network grapevine. He was already supplying CBS with one hit show, *My Favorite Martian*, which had hit Nielsen's Top Ten list during its freshman season. After a long career in the medium (*Sky King*, Ann Sothern's *Private Secretary*, and *The Lone Ranger*), Chertok knew the score and how to win the game. He recalled an idea dreamed up by his writer friend Leo Guild about a female robot, and promptly put to work the writing team of Al Martin and Bill Kelsay to tailor the idea to the talents of Miss Newmar. By early 1964, CBS had bought the idea, now titled *My Living Doll*, and on March 16, put it into its fall schedule.

The show lacked a leading man. Tests were ordered, with Jerry Van Dyke and Richard Long as the favorites. Newmar preferred Van Dyke. For a time, the network considered having both of them as Julie's costars. Instead of one psychiatrist character, why not a team of shrinks? Van Dyke said no to this possibility, preferring to wait until he could headline his own show (he didn't wait long enough; the next year he opted to star in *My Mother, the Car*). Aubrey soon sent down word from the tower that the show needed a "name and forget about the two leading men idea."

Enter Robert Cummings, with ten years of TV performances under his belt (*My Hero, Love That Bob,* and *The Bob Cummings Show*) and he quickly signed to portray the role of the psychiatrist in whose care the robot Newmar is entrusted. Suddenly it was no longer Julie's show.

From the moment the cameras began to roll at the Desilu Gower Street lot, Cummings and Newmar saw things differently. She the method actress, he the old line pro. Sparks flew almost constantly until the pair exploded in early January 1965 with Cummings walking off the set and lot, and never coming back. There were still five episodes of *My Living Doll* yet to film.

A Hollywood reporter described the turmoil: "The thing had been building all season. It was a case of a tense young actress and the veteran who thinks he wrote the book. Cummings showed her how to play the scenes; she burned. On one occasion, she left for a long weekend at Big Sur, claiming she needed a rest from 'people who tell you how to act.' " That about did it. Cummings took a walk, and with it threw away a bundle of money. Julie's instant reaction: "I feel so refreshed. Everyone on the set is terribly, terribly happy."

About a month after the incident, CBS chose to cancel the show anway, the decision coming on the heels of Jim Aubrey's ouster as president of the CBS network. It had nothing to do with Cummings's exit. The ratings were slipping, and the series had become something of a joke in the industry.

Newmar continued to defend the show and her character right up to cancellation: "As I play Rhoda, she is coming closer to the ideal in humanity, and the humans around her are becoming more-and more like robots."

Isaac Asimov, the renowned writer of science fiction and fact, made this statement about Julie Newmar's character, Rhoda: "She is a poorly designed robot who must receive very careful treatment and very sensitive handling if she is to flourish."

We feel the same way about the show.

MY MOTHER, THE CAR

THE GUILTY PARTIES

Creators:	Allan Burns, Chris Hayward
Producer/Director:	Rod Amateau
Co-Producer of Pilot:	Norman Henry
Cameraman:	Charles Van Enger
Film Editor:	Richard Brockway
Music Composed and Conducted by:	Ralph Carmichael
Casting:	Tom Jennings

A Cottage Industries, Inc. production in association with United Artists Television for NBC-TV.

Starring Jerry Van Dyke as Dave Crabtree, Maggie Pierce as Barbara Crabtree, the voice of Gladys Crabtree (a/k/a Mother) by Ann Sothern, Avery Schreiber as Captain Bernard Manzini, Cindy Eilbacher as Cindy Crabtree, and Randy Whipple as Randy Crabtree.

Debuted Tuesday, September 14, 1965, 7:30 P.M. E.D.T. on NBC-TV.

THE FORMAT

Everyman Dave Crabtree (Jerry Van Dyke) is a fairly successful lawyer in a small California town. One day, while browsing used-car lots for a family station wagon, he stumbles upon his mother (dead since 1948, we're told). Dear old Gladys has returned to terra firma as a decrepit 1928 Porter touring car (license plate PZR 317). Yes, a car.

"Hello, son," Mom says, the voice (Ann Sothern's) emanating from the antique car radio. "It was the only way I could find to bring me back." Without so much as even considering a late-model Edsel or Corvair, Dave promptly plunks down $200 and drives Mom home.

Wife Barbara (Maggie Pierce) is properly furious when she gets a gander at the rusting wreck of a car which Dave nonchalantly introduces as his mother. Since no one but Crabtree can hear Mom's voice, Barbara has good reason to worry about her husband's sanity, or lack of it. Hoping to change her feelings toward the car—and his mother—Dave takes the junky jalopy to a custom-body shop for a full overhaul and facelift. Still, wife and kiddies (Cindy Eilbacher and Randy Whipple) hate the heap, until antique car collector Captain Bernard Manzini (Avery Schreiber) offers $1,500 for it. The profitable deal is pooh-poohed. Dave: "A guy couldn't live with himself if he sold his own mother." No argument there, folks.

Of course, Barbara is mad at Dave for not turning the lemon into a goldmine until she realizes that the longer they hold out, the higher Manzini's price will go (the wealthy auto buff has acquired every type of car ever made but one—the 1928 Porter). In the pilot ("Come Honk Your Horn"), Manzini has hired the three greatest crooks in the world to steal the Porter, but their plot is, alas, foiled.

And for the next twenty-nine episodes, the charade continues, with Mother and Son as the focal point of the irrational relationship. She honks her horn petulantly, smacks him on the ass with a smart swing of her front door, turns right when he signals left, backfires and boils over when she's mad, even blows her bloody gasket when the mood strikes. And, get this—she suffers from "carthritis."

In spite of all this childish behavior (the producers knew who their audience was!), Dave scrubs her back, worries about her high oil pressure, keeps her in snug-fitting fan belts, even takes her to a drive-in movie on her birthday.

"Look, Mom, it's great having you back," Dave says in the premiere episode. "I just don't understand why you thought all this was necessary."

We agree.

MEMORABLE MOMENTS

■ "What Makes Auntie Freeze?"—As Dave drives up to the mountains, his mother gets higher and higher from the alcohol in her antifreeze.

■ "I Remember Mama, Why Can't You Remember Me?"—A collision with a truck leaves Mother with amnesia and Dave with a problem, how to bring back a car's memory.

■ "The Incredible Shrinking Car"—Captain Manzini offers Dave a last chance to sell his antique car before using a molecular compressor to shrink it to the size of a small toy.

CLASSIC DIALOGUE

MOTHER: "I understand there's a baseball team called the Mets. If that's possible, I'm possible."

MAGGIE: "It's four o'clock in the morning and you're watching a test pattern."

DAVE: "I know, but I want to see how it ends."

SOME KIND WORDS FROM...

Cleveland Amory of *TV Guide:*
"... the only thing funny about it is not the idea, but the idea that it *was* an idea for a whole television show. In other words, it's just one joke less than a one-joke show...."

The Evening Outlook, Santa Monica, California:
"Poor concept, poor acting, poor entertainment; poor Jerry Van Dyke.... It's awful ... pure gunk."

Jack Gould of the *New York Times:*
"Stalled comedy.... The premiere [episode] made a strong case for not fastening your seatbelts."

Jerry Van Dyke played a small-town lawyer whose late-lamented Mom rein-CAR-nated herself as an old jalopy.

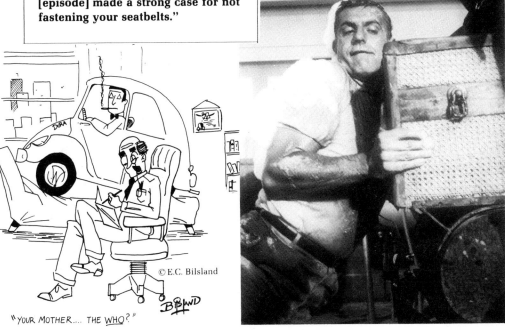

© E.C. Bilsland

"YOUR MOTHER.... THE WHO?"

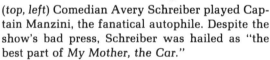

(*top, left*) Comedian Avery Schreiber played Captain Manzini, the fanatical autophile. Despite the show's bad press, Schreiber was hailed as "the best part of *My Mother, the Car.*"

(*top*) Maggie Pierce played Barbara Crabtree, daughter-in-law of a 1928 Porter (actually a 1927 Pierce Arrow, but who cares?).

(*center*) When asked why she was doing the series, Miss Sothern replied: "I'm interested in money!" She bought a new Rolls-Royce that year.

(*bottom*) Jerry Van Dyke: "It's the kind of a series we could have done just as well without the car. But you need something to attract the teenagers these days. So the car became the instrument that gets me into trouble. Aside from the talking car, we played it pretty straight."

"She'll blow her ra-di-a-tor
When things aren't go-ing right,
And when ev-er she gets lone-ly,
We all got-ta spend the night with a car."

Words and Music by Paul Hampton
© 1965, United Artists Music Co., Inc.

FROM THE HORSE'S . . . (Jerry Van Dyke)

Q: What did you think of *My Mother, the Car* when it was first presented to you?
A: I never had faith in the show. I took it because no one was offering me any-thing else. It should have been about me, not a car. Frankly, I was misled about the concept.

Q: Once you were committed to doing the series, how did you feel?
A: My wife and I were happy, we were going to settle down for the first time in our lives. But it was worse than all our years on the road. . . . I was unhappy about the scripts but I found out that when you take a series, that's it. You have no say about anything. You're just the guy who catches the blame when the show folds. Let's face it. If you have a bad series and bad scripts, you're going to look bad.

THE BUSINESS BEHIND THE BOX

My Mother, the Car, the sitcom NBC touted as "a great comedy vehicle" before the show premiered, was bought from Cottage Industries, Inc., a production company, and scheduled in mid-March 1965 by network programing chief Mort Werner. It was among the fifteen new shows (more than half of the total network lineup) selected for inclusion in NBC's 1965-66 schedule. Believe it or not, *My Mother, the Car* (along with another half-hour comedy, *Please Don't Eat the Daisies*) replaced *Mr. Novak,* a high-quality dramatic series about a dedicated high school English teacher starring James Franciscus and Dean Jagger.

My Mother, the Car was the "creation" (we use the word loosely here) of Allan Burns and Chris Hayward who, a season earlier, had concocted *The Munsters,* a so-so CBS "gimmick" comedy. Who would dream that the man who gave us the disastrous *My Mother, the Car* (Burns) would, five years later, create the landmark Mary Tyler Moore series—but he did, along with James L. Brooks. Under the aegis of producer/director Rod Amateau—late of *The Many Loves of Dobie Gillis*—the series went into production in early June on Stage 8 at the Goldwyn Studios in Hollywood.

The first matter of business was to re-shoot certain parts of the pilot which was used as the premiere segment (an omen, to be sure). "We had some problems when mother was supposed to speak to me," star Van Dyke explained. "Originally, I had to turn on the radio and lean toward the dial to hear her. We changed it so she could speak to me anytime, and loud enough so I could hear her, without cocking an ear. When she started talking, the radio light flashed on." During this revamping, one of the car's rigging wires snapped and cut Van Dyke's neck (another omen).

"Sometimes, I think the show's about a guy *stuck* with a car," he said in an interview just prior to the show's debut. In a way, we can understand why Van Dyke, a likable enough guy, decided to tackle this turkey—his TV career was hardly booming. He had appeared in ten segments of the ill-fated *Judy Garland Show* and hosted a dismal game show, *Picture This.* The only bright spots in his television career were four appearances on brother Dick's sitcom, a huge success. Jerry was hoping to create and star in a comedy similar to Andy Griffith's country classic, but plans went awry. Finally, Van Dyke settled for *My Mother, the Car.*

But why Ann Sothern, a respected motion picture actress and star of a very popular earlier TV series, *Private Secretary,* lowered herself to the depths of TV mediocrity, by providing the voice of a car, is beyond us. (Eve Arden and Jean Arthur actually *auditioned* for the same part!) As Sothern put it, "I took it because it was something I'd never done before—and I've been in every phase of show business except playing fairs." (She would have been better off playing fairs.) When asked about the quality of *My Mother, the Car,* Miss Sothern responded: "If a horse can talk [referring to Mr. Ed, presumably], why not a car?"

The critics felt differently. The show was unanimously panned, and viewers deluged the network with letters of outrage. In and out of the industry, the show became the butt of innumerable jokes about the dismal state of television. Even NBC's own *Get Smart!* series once poked fun at the Van Dyke comedy: "We're going to torture you by making you watch *My Mother, the Car* reruns," a KAOS agent once threatened Maxwell Smart.

The program started out strong when it premiered on September 14, 1965. Both National Arbitron (ARB) and Trendex ratings services deemed it #1 for its time period, beating out *Rawhide* on CBS and *Combat* on ABC. For its second outing, the ratings slipped somewhat, but still the show registered a higher rating than its two network competitors. The initial ratings—pegging *My Mother, the Car* above the powerhouse likes of Ed Sullivan, Andy Griffith, and Lawrence Welk—proved one thing: Viewers just couldn't believe that anything as stupid as *My Mother, the Car* could be on TV. They had to see it for themselves!

By season's end, though, this curiosity had waned. Nielsen placed the sitcom #83 (out of a total of 119 shows) with a 14.9 rating and a 25 share. It did beat out *Camp Runamuck* which came in #110.

New Yorkers were, at least, spared the November 9, 1965, episode of the show titled "TV or Not TV" ("Dave's mother is tired of spending night after night in a dark garage—she wants Dave to buy her a TV set"). The infamous blackout took place that night, just two hours before the show would have aired.

We can be grateful that *My Mother, the Car* was canceled after its first season. The ax fell, officially, at the end of February 1966, and the show was replaced by *The Girl From U.N.C.L.E.*, a dandy little dud with Stefanie Powers and Noel Harrison.

Viewer Mrs. Kay Newcomb summed up her feelings about the show in a letter to the beleaguered NBC. She wrote, "I think *My Mother, the Car* is an insult to both Mother and the car. I have almost quit watching television."

FROM THE PSYCHOLOGIST'S NOTEBOOK

The following are comments from Dr. Charles Ansell, a clinical psychologist, himself a "televoyeur":

"*My Mother, the Car* restates the ancient Oedipal legend, reactivating man's most primitive feelings. The series is a gold mine of psychoanalytic insights, unintended by the producers, but guided by that buried part of the infantile mind which still lives on within an adult mentality.

"Jerry Van Dyke acts out every man's basic dream to conquer the mother and have her to himself. Jerry is in complete possession of his car/mother. She is powerless when he locks the garage door.

"An infant feels that since all his desires are gratified by his mother, he therefore must be powerful. In Jerry Van Dyke and his car, the fantasy of omnipotence is thus subconsciously fulfilled for every viewer."

THE NEWLYWED GAME

THE GUILTY PARTIES

Creators:	Nick Nicholson, Roger Muir
Executive Producer:	Chuck Barris
Producers:	Walter Case, Bill Carruthers, Mike Metzger
Directors:	John Dorsey, Bill Carruthers
Contestant Coordinator:	Bob Edwards
Music by:	Frank Jaffe

A Chuck Barris Production for ABC-TV.
Starring Bob Eubanks as host, and Johnny Jacobs as announcer.
Debuted Monday, July 11, 1966, 2:00 P.M. E.D.T. on ABC-TV.

THE FORMAT

"From Hollywood, the Newlywed Capital of the World, . . . it's *The Newlywed Game!*" heralds announcer Johnny Jacobs, as four happy and smiling couples ride out on stage in a latticework contraption that is supposed to look like little chapels. After each pair is introduced with such trivia as "Couple number one forgot their marriage license and spent the first night of their honeymoon in the back seat of their car," Jacobs introduces host Bob Eubanks, a likable chap who looks more like the deacon of a suburban Mississippi Baptist church than a TV game show host.

With their wives secluded offstage, the husbands are asked a series of questions, each worth five points which, during earlier years, explored such important topics as "How many hairbrushes are there in your house?" Now, for the new "recommended for mature audiences" version, the questions deal with the couple's sex life, using such childish and stupid euphemisms as "whoopee session."

"Does your wife like her hot dogs fat and juicy, or small and skinny?" goes one suggestive stumper. Another questionable query: "In a swimming pool, are your wife's bazooms sinkers or floaters?"

After a break for commercials "the wives are reunited with their husbands." With hubby's answers now on cards which he holds in his lap, the questions are repeated so the females can furnish their responses. If they answer correctly— i.e., their responses coincide with those of their husbands—there is the obligatory kiss on the lips, but when they are wrong, which is often, host Eubanks attempts to incite a near riot while remaining undeniably neutral. A wife may slug her spouse with her fist or threaten action "when we get home" ("Did you have to say that on the air??? I *never* wore falsies in my life!"). The contestants are putting on a show, and they know it. The producers admittedly favor the ladies who will systematically pout, sigh, and become thoroughly exasperated on camera when they lose a lousy five points.

The roles are now switched, with the husbands offstage and the wives bombarded with the embarrassing queries. The ante is doubled to ten points for each correct answer. Finally, it is time for the big twenty-five-point bonus question. Here's where they separate the dolts from the dumbbells. With a newly discovered sincerity, Eubanks asks such questions as, "How many large rocks are there on your property?" (This is an all-important query.)

Whichever couple winds up with the most points (if there is a tie, each couple brings forth a card on which they have predicted their final score, without going over) is awarded a "prize selected especially for you," usually a stove, or stereo, or sofa. The prizes are all pretty rinky-dink and somewhat anticlimactic. Chuck Barris, the show's mentor and executive producer, justifies the meager grand prize by rationalizing: "We purposely stay away from big prizes. If we introduced yachts or cars, it would be horrible. They'd kill each other."

He's probably right, but we're surprised gameman Barris hasn't considered such a spinoff.

A TREASURY OF *NEWLYWED GAME* QUESTIONS

What was the last thing your husband did in the kitchen? Put something in or take something out?

What animal would you compare your mother-in-law to?

Would your wife say she sleeps with her toes pointing toward the wall, ceiling, or floor?

On your first date, did your wife act like she had downed a quart of (1) numb rum, (2) fighter cider, (3) zap sap?

What vegetable would your husband most like to sit on?

How many times on an average does your husband masticate?

How does your wife lick her ice-cream cone? Up and down, or around in a circle?

Creator and godfather of *The Newlywed Game,* Chuck Barris, now star of his own vehicle, *The Gong Show:* "You can be so distasteful that people will not watch. There's always a lunatic fringe that always will watch, but you don't want just them."

The pilot, titled *The Newlyweds,* featured three recently married couples. ABC changed it to *The Newlywed Game,* so it wouldn't sound like a soap opera and instructed Barris to add a fourth pair of mates.

SOME KIND WORDS FROM ...

Lee Margulies of the *Los Angeles Times:*
"Tripe. . . . An insult to the sensibilities and a low-water mark on TV's achievement pole."

Charles Sopkin in *Seven Glorious Days, Seven Fun-Filled Nights:*
"It defies description."

Cleveland Amory of *TV Guide:*
"If there is one thing you can say for this show, it is not fixed. It couldn't be."

Born in Flint, Michigan, educated at San Francisco State College where he majored in radio and TV, Bob Eubanks was a disk jockey before becoming a TV host. In the fall of 1965, he presided over a short-lived game show, an updated version of *Jukebox Jury* called *Hit Or Miss*. Aside from that experience, he claims, "Everything I set out to do turns out happily for me."

Bob Eubanks is telling actor Ed Mallory (Dr. Bill Horton on *Days of Our Lives*) that, as a concert promoter, he presented the Beatles to Los Angeles. Mallory was one of a score of celebrities who appeared on *The Newlywed Game* during its early years.

Eubanks seems to enjoy his role as referee to a panel of bickering mates. He claims it's the key-hole peeping urge in us all that makes *The Newlywed Game* so popular.

Two on the Aisle . . . to ensure a fast getaway.

"From Hollywood, heeeeere come the newlyweds! Yes, it's *The Newlywed Game* and now let's meet our newlywed couples for today. . . ." One newspaper critic, echoing the sentiments of many of his colleagues, called it, "Pap in the afternoon."

FROM THE HORSE'S . . . (Chuck Barris)

Q: What are your opinions concerning the state of television?

A: The thing I'm concerned about in commercial TV is its inability to raise itself up, and it never will raise itself up because it doesn't work that way. They're loath to try new forms. I'm not the first person to complain about that and I won't be the last. And I don't care anymore.

Q: Is that the reason for a lack of pioneering spirit in your own programing?

A: The point is, you start out and you're hungry to get something on the air. You get something on. It's the human factor, you're happy. You're happy to be making money and not starving to death, and you're happy to be presenting something that people by and large enjoy—and if great big numbers of people didn't enjoy it, it would be off the air.

Q: How about after that first show gets on the air and succeeds? Can't you then afford the risk of taking chances with new forms?

A: After you have a few shows on, your needs change. You find you'd like to set your own criteria and values. You find that you just can't do that in commercial television as it's set up. So, you get pissed off and you leave, or you don't get pissed off but simply say that's the way it is.

THE BUSINESS BEHIND THE BOX

"*The Newlywed Game* . . . is stupid and mawkish," admitted the man responsible for foisting it on the American public, Chuck Barris. Today Barris can afford to put down his own shows: He is a millionaire many times over, is host of TV's godawful *Gong Show,* and is holder of, as they say in the business, a proven track record. Not bad for a guy who, a year before *Newlywed* went on the air back in 1966, had exactly seventy-two dollars to his name, not enough to buy even a secondhand gong these days.

Called a "cross between Caligula and Soupy Sales" by *TV Guide,* Chuck Barris began his TV production unit with a $20,000 loan from his stepfather David Bortin (repaid three times over). During the gestation period in 1964–65, Barris spent his days in a $25-a-month rented office in Beverly Hills, alternately reading a book about JFK and dozing. He had a proposal for a show called *The Dating Game* circulating around the networks; he once was West Coast head of daytime programing for ABC. Suddenly, his ex-employer knocked on his meager door. They needed a quickie "strip" show (five-days-a-week) to replace *The Young Set,* a faltering talk show starring Phyllis Kirk, late of *The Thin Man.*

With a hurriedly assembled staff of thirteen, Barris put together his first effort, and ABC threw it on the air December 20, 1965. It was an overnight hit, making an instant celebrity of host Jim Lange. Barris had struck gold his first time out; not bad for a guy whose sole success was writing the song "Palisades Park" for Freddy Cannon in 1962.

Next on the network docket was a replacement for *Confidential for Women,* an afternoon pseudo-serial languishing at the bottom of the daytime charts. Barris was ready with a second creation, *The Newlywed Game,* and ABC premiered the lightweight entry on Monday, July 11, 1966, with the successful *Dark Shadows* as its lead-in.

Lambasted by critics (the *Los Angeles Times* called it "a crass and contemptuous depiction of human beings"), the man-versus-woman format of *Newlywed* had undeniable mass-audience appeal. Suddenly "Mr. Nobody of 1965" was somebody: the hottest new producer in Hollywood. Within three short years, Barris was reputedly worth $8 million, a tidy sum, indeed, to amass from, as he himself calls it, "popcorn for the mind."

"Game shows fill a need," says Barris, a wiry fellow in his late forties. "They entertain without making any demands. You don't have to worry about plot. You can come in or leave at any point.

"Frankly, I don't have a high regard for the great wash of any population," Barris continues. "I think they don't want to be educated or informed. They just want to be entertained to the lowest common denominator."

Currently airing in 125 markets, *The Newlywed Game* was syndicated after going off the ABC network at the end of 1974. Like its sister show, *The Dating Game,* it went nighttime six months after debuting as a daytime program, reaping additional millions for Barris and his Chuck Barris Productions, Inc. stockholders. Barris was netting about $50,000 a month from *Newlywed* alone.

Barris is not without his share of problems, however. In 1973, Morris Lempert filed a $20 million lawsuit claiming that the ideas for both *The Newlywed Game* and *The Dating Game* were his. The outcome is still pending, although Barris vigorously contends that both shows sprang from his mind.

What started out merely as a cute and innocuous bit of TV fluff for bored housewives has now blossomed somehow into a trashy and demeaning voyage into voyeurism. Bickering and snickering are the order of the daily proceedings, all of it tasteless.

Barris once created a show called *Greed.* "The idea was that we'd have a panel of four people and present them with a problem," he swears. "We would bring out a dog and a boy and say, 'How little would you take to take the dog away from the boy and shoot it?' Lowest bid took the job and won the money. Or we'd bring out an arthritic old man on crutches and say, 'Who will kick the crutches out from under this gentleman?' People would watch it, believe me."

ABC passed on the idea, claiming in a memo: "It smacks too much of *Let's Make a Deal.*" Instead, Barris came up with *The Gong Show.*

"Somebody called me the king of slob culture," Barris says. "How do I answer that? It doesn't mean anything."

O. K. CRACKERBY

THE GUILTY PARTIES

Creators:	Abe Burrows, Cleveland Amory
Executive Producer:	Rod Amateau
Producers:	Norman Henry, Charles Stewart, Elliott Lewis
Directors:	Rod Amateau, Abe Burrows, David Nelson, et al.
Writer:	Abe Burrows, et al.
Cameraman:	Charles Van Enger
Film Editor:	Richard Brockway
Music by:	Ralph Carmichael
Theme Song by:	Robert Bennett Dolan, Abe Burrows
Casting:	Tom Jennings

A Cottage Industries, Inc. production in association with Beresford Productions, Wayfarer Enterprises, and United Artists Television for ABC-TV.

Starring Burl Ives as O. K. Crackerby, Hal Buckley as St. John Quincy, Brooke Adams as Cynthia Crackerby, Brian Corcoran as O.K., Jr., Joel Davison as Hobart Crackerby, Laraine Stephens as Susan Wentworth, Dick Foran as Slim, and John Indrisano as the chauffeur.

Debuted Thursday, September 16, 1965, 8:30 P.M. E.D.T. on ABC-TV.

THE FORMAT

The Tycoon, a 1964 ABC entry starring Walter Brennan as a misunderstood millionaire industrialist, sank in the sea of deposed sitcoms in 1965. Before the eulogies were even read, the same network announced plans to trot out *O. K. Crackerby,* a show about the richest man in the world who is—you guessed it—

misunderstood. "It must be said of the ABC network," commented a writer in the *Los Angeles Times,* "that it doesn't give up easily."

Burl Ives plays the rough-and-ready Oklahoman (hence his nickname) O. K. Crackerby, who has made his fortunes from a string of gushing oil wells. He's come up the hard way—a ploy to gain sympathy from the audience—and now that he's made it big, his goal in life is to help the less fortunate—who constitute just about everybody left on the planet if we're to believe the "world's richest man" premise. If anything or anyone stands in O.K.'s way, he buys it or him or her. It's as easy as that—a simple man with a heart of gold, . . . and a wallet to match.

Aside from his good deeds, Crackerby is bent on injecting himself and his three motherless kids, Cynthia (Brooke Adams), Hobart (Joel Davison), and O. K., Jr. (Brian Corcoran), into the upper crust of the social set, but he soon discovers that he and his unpolished brood are not welcome in the genteel circle, "the mob," as he calls it. This is precisely the kind of program thesis that invites the reaction, "Who cares?" Who really gives a damn about the world's wealthiest folks? Who cares if they make it in "Society" or not?

Apparently Burl Ives felt otherwise. For years he turned down series offers, but when *O. K. Crackerby* came along he changed his mind. Explaining his role in the show, Ives said, "I want to give my kids a little 'couth,' so I try to buy a Harvard graduate, St. John Quincy [Hal Buckley] as a tutor." Quincy is a penniless but brainy sort who is not particularly impressed by his boss' bundle (neither are we), but takes on the challenge for a lark.

"Somebody," Crackerby tells St. John (pronounced *Sin*-Jin), "gotta teach them those stupid little niceties to help them get in." "In what?" asks the stupefied tutor. "Society." "What's society?" "Whatever I ain't in," pronounces O. K. firmly. With Quincy around to keep him "socially correct," Crackerby travels from one society playground to another, waging his battle against snobbery.

Although Rick DuBrow, a pretty astute UPI writer, conceded that the show had "modest possibilities," for us, *O. K. Crackerby* missed the mark on every level, particularly the most basic one: sympathy. It's just plain impossible to get worked up over a man who's listed on the stock exchange and complains about not being in the Social Register.

MEMORABLE MOMENTS

- Crackerby pulls out all the stops to locate an attractive woman he has met at the airport.
- A Middle Eastern sheik sends Crackerby a harem girl.

- Crackerby's nephew has no head for business: he has purchased 1,000 cuckoo clocks—which he must sell before he can marry the girl of his dreams.

- Crackerby finds himself the owner of a movie studio beset with a major problem—a temperamental star.

- Determined to join a men's club, Crackerby chooses the Tarriers—a club so exclusive that it has only three members.

"He's a diamond in the rough," the ABC publicity machine churned out. "Turn on the hilarity," the network squealed. Viewers by the millions tuned out after they got a good look at *O. K. Crackerby.*

"Tom Moore saw me in a beach commercial and it was mostly my back that showed. I think it must have put on a *marvelous* performance," said actor Hal Buckley about his association with *O. K. Crackerby.* He once did twenty-four commercials in a single year.

Burl Ives as the lead character O. K. Crackerby. The pilot for the show was written by Abe Burrows from an idea by Cleveland Amory. They never actually sat down together and worked out the scripts, and it showed.

Laraine Stephens played tutor Quincy's girlfriend, Susan Wentworth. A few seasons later, she lucked out with *Bracken's World,* which stayed on the air all of two years.

SOME KIND WORDS FROM ...

Harry Harris of the *Philadelphia Inquirer*:
". . . Nothing has appalled us as much as the premise . . . that money can buy everything."

The *Hollywood Reporter*:
"Forced humor. . . ."

Hal Humphrey of the *Los Angeles Times*:
"Not too convincing, . . . and not too funny."

What was reported to be "the happiest set in town," turned out the most ordinary sitcom of the day. Burl Ives could not rise above scripts that were turned out by writers who never saw the original treatment for *Crackerby* as written by *TV Guide* critic Cleveland Amory.

FROM THE HORSE'S ... (Burl Ives)

Q: How did you get involved with this project in the first place?

A: I had just finished reading *Only You, Dick Daring* [a book by Merle Miller about his harrowing experience working on a TV pilot for CBS] and that scared me off some. But when Cleveland Amory, who created *Crackerby*, sent me the script, and I found it to be so good, I changed my mind.

Q: What happened between the conception and the cancellation?

A: We had a succession of different producers and directors and, frankly, the show never did get off the ground in the script department.

Q: Have you found this to be indicative of the general climate in television?

A: Television is no different from any other medium of theatrical communications. Like the others, it has its merits, and after *Crackerby*, I gave it another shot with *The Bold Ones* which was a very nice experience that lasted three years.

THE BUSINESS BEHIND THE BOX

At a time when ABC was agonizing about its weak lineup—*The Jerry Lewis Show*, *Breaking Point, 100 Grand,* to name just a few—its director of program development, Douglas S. Cramer, was entertaining *TV Guide*'s resident critic Cleveland Amory. "I have an idea for a show," Amory informed Cramer, "called *Saturday Review,* a *real* magazine of the air that would handle the arts—books, theater, movies, even TV itself."

Not particularly impressed, Cramer suggested a show about Society, the so-called elite "400," a subject about which Cleveland Amory is an expert. Amory, eager to try his creative hand at TV writing (as opposed to his writing about TV), dreamed up a half-hour situation comedy idea called *My Man St. John,* described in an article in *TV Guide* as the story of "a lovable old millionaire from Oklahoma named O. K. Crackerby, a man with a fortune in natural gas, . . . a widower with three children, a man who has come East to ply the Eastern resort circuit, since he promised his 'missus,' before she passed on, that someday he would stop just making money and do right by the kids."

Everyone who mattered was ecstatic—even the president of the ABC network, Leonard Goldenson, who ordered a pilot, asking Amory, "Are you going to write this show for us?" "No," Amory reportedly said. "I think it would have to be me and someone else."

The someone else recruited by ABC was Abe Burrows, the well-known Broadway playwright (*Guys and Dolls, Cactus Flower,* etc.), the theater's master play doctor. Amory was properly thrilled, even though he realized that he had to relinquish a few of his "points" (show business parlance for percentages) to Burrows. The writer knocked out a thirty-nine-page pilot script, based on Amory's thesis, and the latter read and liked it. Everything was rosy and getting rosier.

Then, when Burl Ives' name was mentioned as a strong contender for the Crackerby role, all parties concerned began mentally spending the money this show would undoubtedly reap. Ives—an Academy Award winner for his role in *Big Country,* the man who had played "Big Daddy" on Broadway in *Cat on a Hot Tin Roof* for more than fourteen months—playing O.K. Crackerby meant that victory was assured. Of course, the title had to be changed from *My Man St. John* to *O. K. Crackerby* to satisfy Ives, but that was all right. Even Cleveland Amory acquiesced and in the same breath gave up a few more points to Ives.

For the role of the tutor, the deposed St. John Quincy, ABC cast an unknown actor, Hal Buckley. Buckley, who was making a pretty fat living acting in TV commercials ($80,000–$100,000 a year) had attended Harvard himself.

By now, *O. K. Crackerby* had become a joint venture with United Artists Television because Ives was under contract to them to do a pilot about sailing in the Caribbean. A black and white pilot of *Crackerby* was shot at the Sam Goldwyn

Studios in Hollywood, and the filming went without incident. When the show was audience-tested, it proved to be the highest of *all* the year's proposed new shows! No fewer than thirty-seven sponsors were lined up to view the masterpiece. ABC invited a Bristol-Myers man and his ad agency representative, Bud Barry, to a closed screening. The pair settled into their seats and the film came on. Ten minutes later, Barry took out a slip of paper, wrote on it, and handed it to his client. The note read: "Buy it." So it was that more than $10 million in new business was brought to ABC because of *O. K. Crackerby*.

The premiere episode—the pilot—aired the night of September 16, 1965, the same evening America got a first glimpse at *Laredo, Mona McCluskey,* and *The Long, Hot Summer*. The opening night ratings could have been better: Arbitron pitted it in last place with a 15.1 rating. *My Three Sons*, the competition, had a 19.3. Reviewers were mixed in their reaction to the show, and most critics panned it.

By this time Cleveland Amory was agreeing with the majority of his newspaper critic colleagues: He didn't like *O. K. Crackerby* either. Week after autumn week, the show went downhill. By the fourth outing, there was not a trace of Cleveland's original idea in evidence. The free-lance writers assigned to hack out the scripts seemed to be happy just to unload whatever material was collecting dust at the bottom of their desk drawers.

Amory's satire of the whole social scene in Palm Beach, Newport, and other points social was now nothing more than a third-rate version of *The Ann Sothern Show*. It was inevitable, we suppose, what with the shenanigans going on behind the scenes. By mid-summer—a month before the first show aired—there had been major firings of top-echelon staffers. Producer Charles Stewart explained why *he* ran afoul of his bosses: "I didn't please all of them. This show had more chiefs than Indians! I was like the manager of a baseball team. You can't fire the team so you fire the manager."

By the end of October, *O. K. Crackerby* had gotten the ABC ax. It was a mercy killing. America was being spared any more than the first seventeen dull stories, the last of which was telecast January 6, 1966. It placed #91 out of the 119 shows of the 1965–66 season. The following week ABC gave us *The Double Life of Henry Phyfe,* a sitcom spoof of spy shows starring Red Buttons. It, too, lasted seventeen weeks, but placed decidedly better than *Crackerby* in the final season list, in sixty-third place.

O. K. Crackerby suffered the slings and arrows of outrageous network tampering. Too many cooks spoiled Amory's original concept, which had enough intrinsic charm to make it click. When will the heads of TV networks butt out, and stop trying to be night school creative-writing instructors?

THE PRUITTS OF SOUTHAMPTON

THE GUILTY PARTIES

Creator:	David Levy (based on the novel *House Party* by Virginia Rowans, a/k/a Patrick Dennis)
Executive Producer:	David Levy
Producers:	Everett Freeman, Nat Perrin
Directors:	Gene Nelson, Oscar Rudolph, et al.
Writers:	Elon Packard, Lou Derman, Fred Freeman, Lawrence J. Cohen, Bart Andrews, Everett Freeman, Stanley Roberts, et al.
Cameraman:	Harkness Smith
Film Editors:	Jor Harrison, Douglas Hines
Music by:	Vic Mizzy
Casting:	Bill Tinsman, Mercedes Manzaneres

A Filmways, Inc. production in association with Phil Dil Productions for ABC-TV.

Starring Phyllis Diller as Phyllis (Mrs. Poindexter) Pruitt, Reginald Gardiner as Uncle Ned, Pam Freeman as Stephanie Pruitt, Gypsy Rose Lee as Regina Wentworth, Grady Sutton as Sturgis, Lisa Loring as Suzy Pruitt, John McGiver as General Cannon, Richard Deacon as Thomas Baldwin, Hope Summers as Gigi, Marty Ingels as Norman Krump, Billy DeWolfe as Vernon Bradley, and Del Moore as narrator.

Debuted Tuesday, September 6, 1966, 9 P.M. E.D.T. on ABC-TV.

THE FORMAT

On September 26, 1962, *The Beverly Hillbillies* went out over the airwaves, and soon became the most popular show on the air. The story of a poor family who struck it rich remained in the top twenty-five for eight of its nine years on the CBS network. It was nominated for four Emmys its first season alone.

So how could a series about a *rich* family striking it *poor* fail?

Phyllis Pruitt (Phyllis Diller) is the widowed matriarch of a dead-broke Long Island society family. With her two daughters, Stephanie and Suzy, and Uncle Ned, she lives what appears to be a normal life, but, in actuality, she's the "guest" of the IRS who has taken over the property for back taxes ($10 million worth). In the opening episode, Tom Baldwin (Richard Deacon) arrives to inform the widow that she is in arrears and will have to move immediately.

The official reason why news of the Pruitts' financial status has been kept quiet is fear of severe repercussions in the business world. (We are told in the opening narration that the Pruitts are on a par with the DuPonts, Rockefellers, and Vanderbilts.) Phyllis has a personal reason why she wants her impecuniousness to remain secret—her feud with next-door neighbor Regina Wentworth (Gypsy Rose Lee) over Phyllis' late hubby. Regina is certain that Phyllis stole him away from her and Phyllis knows that nothing would please the nosy neighbor more than learning that the Pruitts are flat broke.

With every possession they own now attached, the Pruitts must keep up a front, trying to live like millionaires on nothing. In episode after episode, the family manfully tries to restore its former fortune while Phyllis womanfully slapsticks her way through everything from being a secretary to baking pies. After thirteen weeks, it had all worn so thin that viewers couldn't help being on the Government's side. It was a one-joke premise and no one could breathe life into it.

The producers tried by bringing in the likes of Marty Ingels, John Astin, Billy DeWolfe, Louis Nye, and Paul Lynde—a sort of heavyweight comedy repertory company. This helped a little, but not nearly enough. Many felt is was bad judgment to star Phyllis Diller in a sitcom her first time out in TV. She belonged in a variety show format, playing herself. (*The Beautiful Phyllis Diller Show*—a variety show format with Phyllis playing herself—premiered in the fall of 1968. It stayed on the air only half as long as did *Pruitts*.)

As Jack Gould commented sagely in the *New York Times*: "The *Pruitts* makes one appreciate all over again the artistry of Lucille Ball."

We loved Lucy, but apparently we were merely fond of Phyllis.

MEMORABLE MOMENTS

- Phyllis turns private eye to bag the culprits who have stolen the hubcaps off the family Rolls-Royce—and brought a curse down on the house of Pruitt.

- Phyllis, alias Harriet Hammerschlogg, runs afoul of the law when she tries to hock the family heirlooms.

- The Pruitt mansion is a veritable igloo, so Phyllis concocts a scheme to con the Government into repairing the conked-out furnace.

Phyllis Diller's patented laugh got a workout on *Pruitts* as did most of the ancient comedy routines, including this one about a patched-up teabag.

In a last-ditch effort to bolster sagging ratings, the *Pruitts* producers changed the title to *The Phyllis Diller Show* and added a cast of comedy drawing cards, including Marty Ingels (*center*) and Billy DeWolfe. All it did was make the credits longer.

Gypsy Rose Lee played the four-times-married neighbor Regina Wentworth. She couldn't wait to be dropped from the cast so she could devote all her energies to the half-hour talk show she hosted from San Francisco. She didn't have to wait long: Her wish came true in thirteen weeks.

After five years with the fabulously successful *Dick Van Dyke Show,* Richard Deacon signed on to play Tom Baldwin, the unflappable IRS agent, on *Pruitts.* This scene is from the original pilot; note Miss Diller's well-coifed look. Moments like these which depicted her as an elegant grande dame were excised before the series went on the air.

Reginald Gardiner, age sixty-four, played Phyllis Pruitt's Uncle Ned, age eighty-one: "Midway through the show, they changed my role to that of Reggie Pruitt, then a few weeks later, I was Uncle Ned again. I think they were groping a bit, don't you?"

Grady Sutton played the ancient butler Sturgis, one of the few characters from the original *Pruitts* concept to remain relatively intact. He made his film debut in 1924 with Harold Lloyd in *The Freshman,* and later caught the eye of W. C. Fields who cast him in a number of his pictures. *The Pruitts* was Sutton's first and only TV series assignment.

"Television is a challenge. I'd like to succeed just once," admits Phyllis Diller. "I've succeeded in every other area of show business except starring in my own TV show."

FROM THE HORSE'S ... (Phyllis Diller)

Q.   Why did *Pruitts* fail?

A: The cast was all wrong! Pam Freeman, who played my daughter Steffi, was a dancer, not an actress and her role was soon reduced to "Hello, Mom." Grady Sutton [who played Sturgis the butler] was getting old. Even Reggie Gardiner was sick and couldn't take the hot lights. And Gypsy Rose Lee, although a dear dear friend, couldn't do script stuff. She could talk endlessly on her own on any subject, but couldn't stay within the confines of a script.

Q: How about the basic format? Were you satisfied with it?

A: It was a one-joke show. Too full of gimmicks, coming at the end of the "gimmick show" era on TV.

Q: Couldn't you do something about changing it?

A: I worked my ass off on that show. But there was no strength from the beginning. There was never any talk of changing concepts. The last-ditch effort the producers made was too late; the show was already down the tube. Changing the title to *The Phyllis Diller Show* didn't mean a damn thing!

THE BUSINESS BEHIND THE BOX

Phyllis Diller staged her first extemporaneous comedy routine while waiting for her wash to dry in a laundromat in Alameda, California. That was in the early 1950s. By 1955, she was headlining San Francisco's Purple Onion club. In 1958, she had her debut at the prestigious Bon Soir in New York, following it by a triumphant appearance at the hungry i in Frisco. TV beckoned in the early 1960s (although Phyllis made her TV debut with Groucho Marx on *You Bet Your Life*) with a string of stints on Jack Paar's late-night gabfest. Phyllis' self-deprecating put-down humor quickly became the rage of the airwaves. Next stop on the road to stardom: her own television show.

"A series had been my goal ever since I started my career at age thirty-seven," said Ms. Diller shortly after being signed for *The Pruitts of Southampton* in early 1966. "I wanted something permanent, something with which I could build an estate. Playing one-night stands in clubs on the road is no life for a mother with five children to raise."

Pruitts had actually been conceived a half-dozen years before Diller even thought about tossing aside her apron to move in front of the footlights. David Levy, the series executive producer and one-time NBC vice president, recalls: "The series was based on a novel, written by Patrick Dennis (under a pseudonym) of *Auntie Mame* fame, titled *House Party*. Published in 1954, it concerned a pair of sisters who live in this huge mansion on Long Island but really can't afford to. Dennis and I shared the same literary agent, so we eventually became friends.

"I decided to adapt the book for the Broadway stage," continues Levy, creator of TV's *Bat Masterson* series and the man who brought Charles Addams' ghoulish characters to ABC in 1964. "It took me five years to write the play and we were all set to do it with Leland Hayward when my ex-employer, NBC, came to me with a list of dramatic shows they wanted me to produce for them. It was at this juncture that Patrick Dennis gave me carte blanche to do what I wanted with his story in a TV series. I took his wacky characters and molded them into a TV series I called *The Pruitts of Southampton*. I took it to Tom Moore at ABC and he liked it."

Levy had casting difficulties, which delayed the filming of a pilot. He needed not one, but *two* grande dame types for the show, and he couldn't come up with just the right combination. "The lead role was offered to Bea Lillie who was playing on Broadway in *High Spirits*. She had some reservations about doing a TV series, but she loved the concept. In fact, she helped me cast some of the other key roles, including Reginald Gardiner as Uncle Ned. Suddenly, however, she got cold feet and backed out, and I was left without a lead."

When Phyllis Diller became "available," she suddenly had more offers than she could handle. "When a network wants you, every studio in town scrambles to sign you up." Three of them, in fact, fought over her, one paying $10,000 to "hold" her for a few weeks, although the deal fell through.

Armed with a new star, producer Levy found it necessary to change the focus of the concept. He dismissed the early efforts of scripters Lawrence Cohen and Fred Freeman and called in Stanley Roberts and Everett Freeman to tailor *The Pruitts of Southampton* for Phyllis Diller.

"Originally, the character I was to play was a composite of two people—an Auntie Mame-type character. I was an aunt and I didn't like it. How much are you involved if you're not a mother? So they switched it for me," said Diller just a few weeks before the $250,000 color pilot was to be filmed starting February 28, 1966, at General Service Studios in Hollywood, home of Filmways.

The writers tried earnestly to duplicate the Phyllis Diller nightclub persona for the series. Somewhere along the line, however, it went awry. "They made me into a glamorous actress. They kept talking about playing for pathos and getting a tear," says Diller, now approaching age sixty-three. "They had me looking like a pin-up girl with a slick hairdo and an elegant wardrobe befitting Greer Garson. It didn't work."

It worked for ABC, though. A month after the pilot was put together, the network snatched it up, and gave it a berth in their 1966-67 fall lineup. Phyllis was ecstatic: "The show will break all records and win a top Nielsen rating. It's something we haven't had in a long time—an elegant drawing room comedy, grand, chic and low." Ms. Diller was banking on *Pruitts*. She had canceled a full year of lucrative nightclub bookings to portray Phyllis Pruitt, the wealthy Long Island dowager who suddenly finds herself impoverished. "My goal is to make this show an absolute smash."

By the middle of summer, after seven or eight episodes had been filmed, Phyllis was something less than euphoric. Her show seemed no funnier than the departed *Mister Ed,* whose deodorized dressing room she had inherited. She demanded that the pilot be reshot to incorporate "certain elements of my own character." Two full days were spent jazzing up the sample film which was set to air as the premiere episode. Actor Richard Deacon was dismissed and replaced and the character of "Perry Pruitt" was dropped in favor of eight-year-old Lisa Loring playing Suzy, Phyllis' youngest daughter. Pamela Freeman, a dancer on the *Shindig* show, was signed to play daughter Stephanie.

The Pruitts of Southampton premiered Tuesday, September 6, sandwiched between ABC's *Rounders* and *Love on a Rooftop,* and competing with Red Skelton and a major movie on the rival networks. The reviews matched the opening night ratings: both were uniformly poor.

Midway through the season, Filmways admitted they had made some serious conceptual mistakes. They gave Diller greater control of the show, allowing her to revise the Mrs. Pruitt character into a bedraggled, frantic housewife, more like her "real" self. The network even changed the title of the show to *The Phyllis Diller Show,* and moved it to Friday at 9:30 P.M. By then it was too late. The ratings continued to drop. At season's end, *Pruitts* had a 13.8 rating. By comparison, TV's #1 show, *Bonanza,* had a 31.4. ABC mercifully canceled *Pruitts.*

"It was wrong from the start," said Phyllis. "I knew it from the first day of shooting the pilot. But you learn from failure, and it really gives you more confidence in yourself."

Pruitts is available today in syndicated form. It has yet to have any takers.

QUEEN FOR A DAY

THE GUILTY PARTIES

Producers:	Howard Blake, Bill Burch, Ed Kranyak
Packagers:	Robert Temple, Ray Morgan
Associate Producer:	Harry Mynatt
Director:	James C. Morgan
Fashion Commentator:	Jeanne Cagney
Wardrobe Mistress:	Hazel Dewey
Escorts:	Harry Mynatt, Ted Wood

A Queen For a Day, Inc. production for NBC-TV and ABC-TV.
Starring Jack Bailey as host, and Gene Baker as the announcer.
Debuted Thursday, April 28, 1955, 2:30 P.M. E.D.T. on NBC-TV.

THE FORMAT

"It wasn't so bad when my husband Jack died, although he had lingered on for nearly ten years, but it turned out that his life insurance was worthless; the salesman had been a fraud. Then my sister became bedridden with a mysterious illness, and it lasted for seven months. I sold off all the furniture and appliances, which kept things going for a few months, but the night before I was to sell the house it caught fire and burned to the ground. The fire insurance was with the same so-called company as my husband's life insurance policy. I took my kids, John and Linda, and moved into my sister's cramped apartment to consolidate things. One night Linda, who had always been sickly, developed these violent spasms and died before the doctor could get there. Several weeks later. . . ." So goes the average *Queen For a Day* hard-luck lament.

Four luckless but lucky ladies are trotted onstage after being carefully selected by the *Queen For a Day* staffers and host Jack Bailey. Each woman entering the mammoth theater-restaurant has been asked to fill out a "wish card," which contained spaces to write in the answers to: (1) What is your wish if you are chosen Queen? and (2) Why did you choose this? Based on the responses to these two vital questions, Jack and the producers would ferret out twenty-five possibilities, all of whom were quickly interviewed by Bailey before air time. Bailey had a keen eye—he knew who was faking; he knew who would make a good contestant (he *loved* the little old ladies); and he knew if the staff could produce the all-important asked-for wish. From these twenty-five hopefuls, the four main contestants of the day would be chosen to appear on the show, and only one of them would ultimately become Queen for a day.

"Would *you* like to be Queen for a day??" the daily sobfest begins, Bailey posing the perennial question straight into the camera. For the next forty-five minutes, viewers are subjected to a veritable parade of pathos, a Normandy-size invasion of privacy that starts with a bevy of scantily clad girls trotting across the tacky *Queen* set, showing off the gifts of the day—fur coats, dresses, TV sets, washing machines, *ad nauseum,* while an off-camera announcer extols the wonderful virtues of each product or service.

Then host Jack Bailey takes over. Microphone in tow, the man responsible for making Her Majesty's fondest dreams come true—jester of little old ladies, they called him—starts the humiliating interviews. These might not have been so bad on their own (and some of them were *very* bad) had it not been for Bailey's so-called witty repartee. For instance, one housewife wanted a new set of living room furniture. She told us that her old one had been taken away by a man who had come to clean it and had taken it, along with her $100 deposit, never to return. She added, as a postscript, that this fateful event happened on December 31. "Happy New Year!" laughed good old Bailey, sounding decidedly cretinous.

When a Mrs. Margaret Eleck started to cry because she wanted a bedroom set after her house and chicken farm had burned to the ground, Mr. Bailey said appropriately, "Ah, you're called Mrs. Eleck. Well, I'm often called that, too, 'Smart' Eleck!" (Even the commercials reeked of something unsavory. A Queen—now able with a new car to visit her dying husband, paralyzed by a stroke—could also have the pleasure of knowing that she could take him a year's supply of men's deodorant.)

The sick and sordid spectacle winds down as the judging takes place. Like a carnival barker about to herald the crowning of a new prize calf, Bailey holds his extended hand over the heads of each of the four contestants separately, while an audience meter records the response of the 800 or so people in the theater. The chosen Queen, blanched and bawling, would totter imperceptibly, then steady herself as assistants would rush in to swathe her in ersatz ermine and paste jewels, seat her on a tacky velvet throne, and press upon her a bouquet of four dozen roses (thorns removed). Mind you, we never saw the three losers from that moment on; no matter how desperate their needs, and though they surely supplied their share of the "entertainment" they had to settle for a radio, a toaster, or a dozen pairs of nylon stockings. If they dared burst into tears, they were quickly and quietly ushered offstage.

Bailey would pile gift upon gift like a man possessed, making sure the lucky lady's original dream was not forgotten. The following day, at 9:30 A.M., her "day" as Queen officially began. First to a hairdresser, then to lunch at a movie studio or a big Hollywood restaurant, then to a studio tour and a professional makeup job. After a short afternoon rest, she was off to dinner and a show at a local club, and then another club. One short, gay whirl before returning to those same dreary problems.

Queen was vulgar, sleazy, and in just plain bad taste. And that's probably why it was so successful; it was precisely what the public wanted at the time. In the words of H. L. Mencken, "Nobody ever went broke underestimating the taste of the American public."

MEMORABLE MOMENTS

- When asked by Jack Bailey why he wanted a new suit, a little lad said, "I want to wear it tomorrow when Mommy and Daddy get married!" (Luckily, this took place during the pre-telecast interview portion of the *Queen* show.)

- One prospective Queen wanted passage to Africa so she could be a missionary. "What kind of missionary?" asked Bailey routinely. "Independent," snapped the woman. "I want to go into the interior of Nigeria where no one's heard of the Lord."

- "We had one old lady about eighty," recalls king-of-the-queens Bailey, "who wanted a new set of teeth. Seems she played the cornet in Sunday school, but couldn't any more because her teeth were so loose they'd slip off the mouthpiece. We fixed her up with a nice set of uppers and lowers."

SOME SAMPLE "WISH" CARDS

"I'd like a bird for an old lady of ninety-four. She had one but it died and she doesn't realize it. She keeps it in a cage, talks to it, and takes it out and kisses its head."

"My husband needs a new artificial eye because last winter his froze and cracked."

"I need $100 for a divorce. My husband tried to rape my six-year-old daughter, then left with the money and the car. I have to divorce him so I can testify against him in court."

"I could use a new mattress. My husband died in bed two months ago and ruined our mattress."

"My sister was murdered and I have been told she left some money. I need a detective to find out where it is."

"I could use twin beds. My doctor told me I should take it easy."

SOME KIND WORDS FROM ...

Jack Gould of the *New York Times*:
"What hath Sarnoff wrought??"

TV Guide:
"... a chamber of horrors."

Confidential magazine:
"The worst program on the air."

Cleveland Amory:
"It's a bawl."

Prior to his tenure with *Queen For a Day*, Jack Bailey was an actor, radio announcer, and accomplished musician (he plays five instruments). After *Queen* was established as a solid success, he gave up acting, claiming he enjoyed chatting with all the ladies and sharing their miserable stories for two decades.

When *Queen* was canceled in the fall of 1964, Jack Bailey said: "Really, a lot of people don't know that *Queen* is gone yet and in some cases I haven't the heart to tell them." Bailey really *was* a softie; he was one-time quizmaster on *Truth Or Consequences*, but detested dishing out the latter.

Barbara Lyon, one of the *Queen* helpers, holding balloons.

Ed Kranyak started out as a truck driver for the show, was upped to associate producer status several years later, and then achieved the ultimate position, producer. He was often seen on camera, catching fainting Queens or lending hankies to dry many a moist eye.

THE BUSINESS BEHIND THE BOX

There once was a little radio show, a sort of rival to Don McNeill's *Breakfast Club,* titled *Breakfast in Hollywood* starring Tom Breneman. A member of the show's staff, Ray Morgan, was having considerable trouble getting ladies to attend the broadcast. He finally solved the problem by giving each of them a small bouquet of flowers, making every lady feel ... well, like a queen for a day.

"That's it!" Morgan probably said. "A *new* show called *Queen For a Day!*" Borrowing considerably from another radio format, *The Original Good Will Hour* starring the fictional John J. Anthony, *Queen* debuted on the Mutual radio network on April 29, 1945, and was an immediate hit. Host Jack Bailey, one-time voice of Walt Disney's Goofy, was plucked from another Mutual quizzer, a minor bomb called *Stop That Villain* and given the job of, as one wag called it, "hankie holder for harassed housewives." As it turned out, the role held him in good stead—his employment lasted almost twenty years.

Queen was transferred to the tube in the spring of 1955, although it continued to play simultaneously on radio for almost ten years from the day the sob show made its radio debut. Instantaneously, it became daytime TV's all-time biggest hit, with 13 million regular viewers watching every day! Sponsors (there was a waiting list) paid $4,000 for a one-minute commercial, resulting in NBC's annual take of $9 million from this tour into the valley of tears.

The program's wealthy packagers, the aforementioned Morgan and his partner Bob Temple, gleefully made no apology for the pathetic proceedings. *Queen*, they reasoned, was entertainment. A parade of hard-luck housewives, each with a pitiful tale of woe—a dying husband, two or three dying children, a burned-down house—that sort of thing, only keep it light and upbeat. Then, whoever had the most miserable story, according to a heartless applause meter, got to go to dinner at the best restaurant, the theater, nightclubs, your general night-and-day on the town. And gifts—usually $3,500 worth of prizes, a regular windfall of wonderfulness. One lady, whose husband had been out of work for over a year and who had six children below the age of five, received, for example, a lovely set of crystal goblets. That's on a par with giving the neighborhood rabbi a pet pig.

Howard Blake, one of the series of producers *Queen* employed throughout its run, explains: "The money didn't come only from advertisers. It also came from the companies that gave us free merchandise in return for plugs. This money also had to cover the salaries of the girls who modeled the clothes we gave away and who displayed the other wares." Ray Morgan managed $5,000 a week from this fund himself.

"The more gifts we gave to the Queen, the more money we made," continues Blake. "We loaded the gals with gifts—at the rate of about $1 million a year."

The TV version became so super-successful that NBC expanded it from thirty minutes to forty-five by the end of 1955. "Only fifteen of that forty-five minutes," claims Blake, "were left for the actual show—Jack Bailey, the stories, and the voting. The other time was consumed by commercials and plugs." By the end of the 1956–57 season, *Queen* ranked #1 among all prize-giving programs on the air, daytime and nighttime, awarding some $22,500 per week, according to a survey in *U.S. News & World Report*. (*The $64,000 Question* was on the same list, ranking third.)

The program emanated from the Moulin Rouge, a combination theater-restaurant on Sunset Boulevard, a block away from Vine Street. The audience, mostly ladies, came to enjoy the stories that the mistresses of misfortune unraveled, and the $2.10 "*Queen For a Day* Special Luncheon" (an onion sandwich?). The show was anything but fixed. Nothing was faked, nothing ever rehearsed even slightly. The four candidates for Queen were picked purely for their personal stories. The general assumption was that the most needy and deserving were chosen to appear. This was not always the case. If a woman desperately needed a doctor or a lawyer, she was dumped. These services could not be provided because there was no way of telling beforehand how much they might cost. A candidate had to want something that could be plugged—a stove, some carpeting, an artificial leg, a year's supply of baby food, etc.

Sometimes these wishes, as they were called by the Queen staff, were difficult to supply. For example, on one telecast, a chosen Queen wanted a babysitter who could also milk goats. Now you don't find that in the Yellow Pages. But the Queen staffers came up with exactly that combination in one person. Some wishes were downright ridiculous, a sort of mirror of the show itself. A pet skunk? Three tons of hay, a barrel of mud, and 500 fly swatters? How about twenty-five broken watches "for my husband who's taking a correspondence course in watch repair?" We suspect that sometimes contestants were selected on the basis of having the most outlandish and laughable requests.

During Queen's nineteen-year reign of tears on radio and television, some 5,000 Queens wailed their way into the hearts of the program's middle-age audiences, with a total purse exceeding $23 million. The sentimental sojourn into prizeland started dropping off in the ratings war of the late-1950s and was dropped by NBC, only to be picked up by faltering ABC who kept it going another five seasons. But, alas, toward the end, housewives began to show preference for calamity undiluted by the fun-and-games aspect of Queen, with the result that the ratings on soap operas went up considerably. In fact, when Queen was canceled in the early fall of 1964, it was replaced by a soap, The Young Marrieds. Basically, the only missing element of the new show was Jack Bailey.

Putting human misery on display, Queen's stock in trade, could hardly be called humane. It did, we guess, prove to millions that "if you think you've got troubles, you should see the poor women on this show." That's the kindest cut of all.

THE SAMMY DAVIS JR. SHOW

THE GUILTY PARTIES

Producer:	Joe Hamilton
Director:	Clark Jones
Writers:	Buz Kohan, Bill Angelos
Associate Producer:	Carol Kritz
Musical Director:	George Rhodes
Choreographer:	Lester Wilson
Set Designer:	Frank Skinner

A Sammy Davis Jr. production for CBS-TV.

Starring Sammy Davis, Jr., and guest hosts Johnny Carson, Sean Connery, and Jerry Lewis.

Debuted Friday, January 7, 1966, 8:30 P.M. E.S.T. on NBC-TV.

THE FORMAT

"I'm not going to do a variety show," said the five-foot-five showman Davis. "I'm going to do a show with variety. There's a difference—no sketches, no bad jokes. When Richard and Liz come on, he's going to do 'Camelot' and she's going to watch. When Sean Connery comes on, he's going to sing 'There Is Nothing Like a Dame' the way he used to do when he was a chorus boy in London.

"One evening I'll have Louis Armstrong on one side and Ella Fitzgerald on the other," Sammy Davis, Jr. added in a pre-show interview in late 1965. "I want five of the great impressionists and get five James Cagneys going at once. It's not going to be all fun. The pressures are there . . . first Negro with a big show. All I really want to do is handle all of it with swinging dignity."

This optimism was unfortunately misplaced. By the time Sammy Davis made it on the air, his program was nothing more than an hour of uninspired twaddle. That is, if you can be so flattering as to call Elizabeth Taylor whistling a Welsh folk song twaddle—that, by the way, was one of the "highlights" of Sammy's premiere outing, telecast January 7, 1966.

Sammy Davis, Jr.—the consummate performer, the shining star of Broadway's *Golden Boy,* the pride of the Rat Pack—opening his "non-variety show" with the show-stopping tune from *The Roar of the Greasepaint,* "Nothing Can Stop Me Now." Something did: Mr. and Mrs. Richard Burton. The Mister bantered with Davis, exuding an artificial camaraderie as each tried to outdo the other with superlatives plucked from a dictionary.

Despite Sammy's supposed friendship with the Burtons, he was totally ill at ease in their company. In fact, he looked nervous throughout the opening show and most of the other programs he fronted during the series' short run. Also, Sammy is a "hip" artist, and this got in the way of his performances. He exuded little warmth, and gave the impression that he was too sophisticated to be bothering with TV at all. Like Judy Garland before him, Davis did not mix well with guests. He was doing a poor job of convincing the public that he was just plain folks.

When Sammy was performing solo—in fact, he headlined an entire hour—he was nothing less than brilliant. He can hold an audience in the palm of his hand, and do it without peer. But laden with undistinguished production and hokey writing, Davis could not rise above mediocrity. For his last number on the closing show, he sang "What Kind of Fool Am I?" wearing a clown's outfit and a red frightwig. It was a song filled with irony. Davis had allowed himself to be steered in the wrong direction, against his own instincts as a master performer.

"Is there anything distinctive about your show," asked a *New York Times* reporter, "compared to other weekly variety programs?" "Yes," replied Davis. "There's this colored fellow who's the host and star of it!"

"I want to get Olivier to do his great pantomime of Chaplin," said Davis before his show's premiere. "We'll have country and western, Johnny Cash as well as Mel Torme and Ella. The show won't be for hippies only." His program had neither Olivier nor Cash, and was too "hip" to be a hit.

SOME KIND WORDS FROM ...

Hal Humphrey of the *Los Angeles Times*:
". . . badly paced and disjointed."

Cleveland Amory of *TV Guide*:
"It was one of the littlest things ever."

Jack Gould of the *New York Times*:
". . . spiritless and static, . . . totally lackluster and a keen disappointment."

Time magazine:
"As for the much-ballyhooed TV debut of Sammy's big drawing card, Mr. and Mrs. Richard Burton—well, television has rarely seen such a bust."

The one-and-only Nat King Cole, who paved the way for Sammy Davis, Jr., couldn't sustain his own NBC show of the 1950s because of viewer apathy and sponsor indifference. "I think things are different now," said Davis, hoping his own program could attract the interest of both factions.

Jerry Lewis was one of three substitutes for host Sammy Davis, when the latter was contractually barred from headlining his own show. By the time Davis returned from exile the following week, the ratings were already in the cellar.

Sammy performs in one of his ABC specials, this one aired on November 25, 1965. It was his expertise on this and other extravaganzas which caused NBC to offer him his own show.

FROM THE HORSE'S ... (Sammy Davis, Jr.)

Q: It is a well-known fact that you have taken the blame for the demise of the *Sammy Davis Jr. Show.* Why?
A: I'm a downfront performer. I really didn't fit in the living room, so to speak. That was part of it. The other problem was that [NBC] kept saying, "Sammy, you can't do that because this is television," which is somehow different.
Q: What did NBC expect?
A: Another *Hollywood Palace.* They didn't want me to smoke on camera, and told me "no open shirts." But they insisted going in that I run my own show.
Q: Perhaps, then, network interference was to blame.
A: I've got no cop-out. It was nobody's fault but mine. I apologized especially for those first five shows. They were horrible. We never got over that bad beginning—even when we started to swing those last six shows.
Q: Any regrets?
A: The only thing that really hurt me was the way some of the critics rapped Elizabeth Taylor and Richard Burton after the first show. They said she was fat and couldn't sing. Why should Elizabeth Taylor sing, and what kind of reviewing is *that?*

THE BUSINESS BEHIND THE BOX

Back in the 1950s, NBC made what broadcasters considered large strides when it announced the signing of singer Nat King Cole to headline a variety show. There had been prior attempts at black series, but they were either minor affairs like *Sugar Hill Times* in 1949, or silly sitcoms like *Amos 'n' Andy* and *Beulah.*

Nat's show debuted November 5, 1956, as a fifteen-minute interlude after the nightly news. Despite the network's faith and efforts to save it, the show failed to attract a large enough audience to warrant sponsors. It died on December 17, 1957, and, along with it went the immediate future of "black" programing.

Some years later, in 1965, NBC unveiled a dramatic series from the Sheldon Leonard stable. *I Spy* costarred comedian Bill Cosby and ran three seasons, during which time Cosby picked up a trio of Emmys for his outstanding portrayal of Alexander Scott. It was an important milestone; the door had been opened for performers like Sammy Davis, Jr.

On October 27, 1965, Davis signed a thirteen- to eighteen-week contract with NBC, making him the first black to enjoy "the Gleason Treatment." Like "the Great One," Davis was permitted complete control of his show's content and budget, and as executive producer he was free to hire and fire, and pay the salaries of everyone from guest stars to the lowliest crew member. By mid-November, Davis had accomplished something of a coup: He had signed Elizabeth Taylor and Richard

Burton to be his first guests. The much-publicized pair had just turned down half a million dollars to appear on the tube, but accepted Sammy's offer of $50,000 for the variety stint (which they turned over to a charity). It was a gracious favor from friends.

"My whole belief," said Davis in a pre-show interview, "is that the more we can work with people we know personally, the more we can set up a rapport that'll give the show a point of view. With people like Sinatra, Dean Martin, and Liz and Dick, there's a closeness. If I'm on the show with people I admire, I just feel comfortable."

Why hadn't the multitalented Davis plunged into the lucrative confines of weekly television before? "Basic and to the point—no one offered me," said Davis who earlier had a deal with ABC to do a group of specials. One of them, *Sammy and His Friends,* starring Frank Sinatra, Count Basie, and Edie Adams, had been taped before Davis' deal with NBC had even been discussed. Tom Moore, network president of ABC, was more than a little annoyed with Sammy about his "defection" to the enemy. And to show his displeasure, Moore decided to hold Davis to one of the fine-print clauses in his contract which called for the performer *not* to appear on a rival network three weeks before and one week after the airing of the special, set for February 1, 1966.

Obviously this caused quite a problem. Here was Davis, all set to premiere his NBC extravaganza on January 7, 1966, with the Burtons as special guest stars, and he was being placed in a contractual straitjacket for the next four weeks. He rationally suggested to NBC that it hold off the debut until after February 8, but the network brass told him they thought the "oddity" of this arrangement might even work to his advantage.

It didn't. The show made its scheduled debut in the time slot previously held by *Convoy,* a failing military drama starring John Gavin.

Though critics were nearly unanimous in their apathy, the opening night ratings were predictably fantastic—but it's hard to know how many tuned in to see Sammy and how many to ogle Mrs. Burton's ampleness. One thing was certain: Critics by the score complained that Sammy did not participate enough in his own show, that he was little more than a catalyst/host. For a performer as versatile as Davis, this was too restricting. Not only that, but now Davis was faced with the fact that he had to be off his own show for a month.

Johnny Carson, Sean Connery, and Jerry Lewis subbed for Sammy with only routine results. While the star himself did everything he could behind the scenes to energize the efforts, Davis just couldn't overcome the most obvious of shortcomings—his non-presence. The Nielsens, which had started high, were plummeting fast. Those inclined to tune in to see Sammy on his show would tune out when they learned of his absence.

By the time Davis returned to the show, for the February 11 airing, it was too late. While the reviews were decidedly better than those of the premiere, the fact remained that no one was interested any more. Even the performers who had once promised friend Sammy that they would appear—Sinatra, Dino, Joey Bishop, and the like—decided they were "too busy."

When the 1966–67 NBC fall schedule was announced on February 23, *The Sammy Davis Jr. Show* was nowhere to be found. The network dropped it without a formal announcement. Davis was predictably nonplussed. He felt the shows were improving, and had hoped that the ratings would eventually follow suit. NBC pulled the show after the April 22 telecast, replacing it with two-year-old reruns of *Sing Along With Mitch.*

In interviews purporting to explain the show's demise, Davis vowed he would never again do a TV variety show. "If I don't know anything else, I know how to entertain people, but I've got to be me," he explained, referring obviously to NBC's interference. "I want to do dramatic things on TV now. I'm passing up Ed Sullivan and *Hollywood Palace.*"

He didn't stay away long. By 1975, Davis was back on the air with a syndicated variety show. It, too, flopped. Let's hope that someday Davis will return to television on a regular basis with the right format. God knows how much less talented performers have made it in this medium.

SATINS AND SPURS

THE GUILTY PARTIES

Producer/Director:	Max Liebman
Choreographer:	Charles O'Curran
Associate Producer/Director:	Bill Hobin
Book by:	William Friedberg, Max Liebman, with Neil Simon, Will Glickman, Fred Saidy
Music and Lyrics by:	Jay Livingston, Ray Evans
Art Director:	Frederick Fox
Musical Director:	Charles Sanford
Orchestrator:	Nelson Riddle
Choral Director:	Clay Warnick
Technical Director:	Heino Ripp
Costumes by:	Paul DuPont
Sponsors:	Sunbeam, Hazel Bishop

A Max Liebman Presents . . . production for NBC-TV.

Starring Betty Hutton as Cindy Smathers, Guy Raymond as Tex, Josh Wheeler as Dirk, Edwin Philips as Ollie, Kevin McCarthy as Tony Bart, Neva Patterson as Ursula, Maggie McNellis as the couturier, Genevieve as the chanteuse, Ray Drakely as the headwaiter, and Joe Ross.

Presented Sunday, September 12, 1954, 7:30 P.M. E.D.T. on NBC-TV.

THE FORMAT

"This is not like the movies," Betty Hutton reasoned a few hours before she made her TV debut in *Satins and Spurs*, Max Liebman's first "spectacular" for NBC. "With a picture, you have time to get set for the blow, to roll with it, good or bad.

153

With this, we'll have the news tomorrow morning. Wouldn't you know it would be a Monday?"

On Monday, September 13, 1954, the news was out, and it wasn't good. In the tradition of Max Liebman's earlier TV hit, *Admiral Broadway Revue, Satins and Spurs* was an "original" musical comedy. But as *Newsweek* pointed out, "The book smacks of *Annie Get Your Gun* or any other saga about a cowpoke in the big city." Of course, that's pretty fair source material, and to have the star of the film version of it is another plus. But . . .

Cindy Smathers (Betty Hutton) arrives in New York to take part in the big rodeo at Madison Square Garden. She's like a fish out of water in the big city. A journalist with *Life* magazine, Tony Bart (Kevin McCarthy), befriends her, hoping to do a big story on her for his magazine. With a song for every occasion, including such forgettable tunes as "I've Had Enough" and "Nobody Cares," and a script doctored by Neil Simon, *Satins and Spurs* was clearly not going to force Irving Berlin into retirement.

Sure, there were some bright spots: Betty Hutton singing the title tune and warbling "Sexy Sadie"; Josh Wheeler and Guy Raymond, playing a couple of cowpokes who take Cindy under their wing; and a terrific show-stopper, "Little Rock Roll."

But it was not the "spectacular" promised. When it ran seven minutes short—a serendipitous happening—Steve Allen, star of the new *Tonight* show, came on to give viewers a "tour" of the "world's largest TV studio," from which the show emanated.

It was the best part of the ninety minutes.

At the Desert Inn in Las Vegas on November 10, 1954, less than two months after *Satins and Spurs* aired, Betty Hutton announced to her closing night audience: "This is my last show—I'm retiring from show business." With tears in her eyes, she bowed long and low while the band played "Auld Lang Syne." She referred to the TV debacle as "that thing we don't talk about," adding, "It could have been much better."

Betty Hutton portrayed Cindy Smathers, a rodeo queen, in Max Liebman's "spectacular," *Satins and Spurs.* Industry trade papers, known in the business as "the ego press," called the production "lavish," adding, "It will be hard to top this one." *Daily Variety* said about Hutton: "She's for TV and TV is for her—the rest of the world should get along so well together."

Kevin McCarthy costarred with Hutton in the show, playing Tony Bart, the *Life* magazine photographer with whom she falls in love.

SOME KIND WORDS FROM . . .

Newsweek:
"A $300,000 letdown!"

The *Hollywood Reporter:*
"A big beautiful hodge-podge . . . a lot of perspiration, but no inspiration."

Arthur Shulman and Roger Youman in *The Television Years:*
"Did not even come close to living up to all the advance publicity. . . ."

TV Guide:
"Spotty. . . ."

THE BUSINESS BEHIND THE BOX

Described as a "practical dreamer," Sylvester (Pat) Weaver created much of the "greatness" NBC achieved during its early years in the medium. It was he who developed the pacesetting *Today* show concept, following it up two years later with *Tonight.* It was also network president Pat who coined the term "TV spectacular," an extravagant ninety-minute production purportedly more superb than a mere "special." The first of these lavish diversions, presented as *The Sunday Spectacular,* was *Satins and Spurs,* an original musical comedy starring Betty Hutton. It was live, aired only once on September 12, 1954, and its saga is worth retelling.

Pat Weaver set in motion his plans to present twenty big-scale concoctions for the 1954–55 season by signing master showman Max Liebman as producer. Liebman, well known and respected as the head man of *Your Show of Shows,* an NBC offering, decided to approach Betty Hutton, a long-time TV holdout, to headline the first spectacular. Miss Hutton was a hot property, having recently starred in the films *Annie Get Your Gun* and *The Greatest Show on Earth,* and Liebman was anxious to work with her. Miss Hutton also wanted to work with Liebman, having long admired his credits. So, by May 15, 1954, it was all set: Betty would make her TV debut on NBC's premiere spectacular. Her salary: $50,000, the highest fee ever paid for a one-shot performance.

With a total budget of $300,000 (the average NBC spectacular cost $150,000 to $175,000), Liebman started producing. His would be the first production to emanate from the mammoth new NBC color studio located in Brooklyn (now the home of the daytime soap *Another World*) that had formerly been the old Vitagraph Studios. His first task, naturally, was to come up with an idea, something special to fill ninety minutes of airtime. With Billy Friedberg, Liebman created a story about a rodeo queen who comes to New York to appear in the annual rodeo at Madison Square Garden. While there, a writer-photographer for *Life* magazine latches onto her, intent on doing a long article on what makes a rodeo star tick. They fall in love, have a spat, and finally get back together again in Act Four.

To add meat to this bone of a concept, Miss Hutton went to Jay Livingston and Ray Evans, a pair of songwriters responsible for such ditties as "Mona Lisa" and "Buttons and Bows." After dreaming up the title *Satins and Spurs,* the songsmiths went to work composing. Betty also approached Alan Livingston of Capitol Records, who agreed to put out an album from the show. Without hearing so much as one song, the record company executive ordered his art department to design the album cover, leaving blanks for the song titles. "They told us not to make the titles too long," recalls Ray Evans, "because they wouldn't fit on the cover." Capitol was planning an album of ten songs that were yet to be written.

Against Max Liebman's wishes, Hutton hired her estranged husband, Charles O'Curran, to stage the show. (Betty had walked out on her Paramount Pictures' contract in 1952 when the studio refused her request that O'Curran direct her next film. He had been the dance director on the film *Somebody Loves Me* before she married him.)

Betty worked hard to get ready for *Satins and Spurs,* going so far as to break in the new songs in a nightclub act in Atlantic City in early August. Said one of her closest friends at the time: "Betty is a perfectionist. When she decides to do something, she goes all out. She rehearsed six weeks for that one TV appearance!"

Satins and Spurs—all "ninety minutes of sparkling entertainment," the newspaper ads promised—was telecast live from New York at 7:30 P.M. on Sunday, September 12, 1954. The color production (although there were fewer than 10,000 color sets in existence) was made up of thirteen scenes in four acts. The ten Livingston-Evans songs were, for the most part, dull.

The reviews were almost uniformly poor, many of them downright scathing. The special Capitol record album of the show's songs laid one of the largest and most embarrassing eggs in recording history. But the most remarkable outcome of the proceedings was Betty Hutton's decision at age thirty-three to retire from show business. "TV is a very exciting medium, but it's not for me. It's great for someone with more energy—it's a medium for the younger crowd," said Hutton two weeks after the show. "And I can't take the heartbreaks any more."

She fully expected *Satins and Spurs* to be a smash hit, despite the predictions along New York's "TV Row," Madison Avenue, that the program "suffered from star temperament." Liebman was forced to compromise his ideas in the face of an understood ultimatum from the Hutton contingent—"Do it our way, or else!" The "or else" meant no show.

When all the furor died down, Liebman made his own brief statement to the press: "It's a long story. All I can say is that I knew in advance what the circumstances would be and I was prepared for them. She brought in her own people to handle certain phases of the production when I would rather have used my own staff."

The Trendex rating for *Satins and Spurs* was a sheepish 16.5 against a whopping 34.6 for Ed Sullivan's *Toast of the Town* tribute to Darryl F. Zanuck.

An advertising agency official for Hazel Bishop, the sponsor, quipped, "We're calling the show *Nails and Coffins*. We were afraid the rating would be low, but we never dreamed it would be that low."

"NBC kept crowing about how much money they were spending on the show," another adman said. "That leaves a bad taste in people's mouths." Some viewers resented the fact that the program was televised in color. Those without color receivers (3,499 out of 3,500 homes) did not want to "waste" time watching a show when the "best thing about it is its color!"

And so "the spectacular" was born—though many television people feel it an unfortunate term. Pat Weaver felt otherwise: "It's just hard to get word to the public about a one-shot show. The great lethargic American masses have lots of other things on their minds."

SUPERMARKET SWEEP

THE GUILTY PARTIES

Executive Producer: David Susskind
Producer/Director: Allan Wallace

A Talent Associates, Ltd., production for ABC-TV.
  Starring Bill Malone as host.
  Debuted Monday, December 20, 1965, 11 A.M. P.S.T. on ABC-TV.

THE FORMAT

Who could imagine that the gluttony of an overstuffed population could be so faithfully mirrored on a modest daytime program? *Supermarket Sweep,* with its race against the clock to see who could tally up the highest grocery bill, featured careening cart-pushers bent on piling up as much junk food, salad dressing, and Tang, as many pot roasts and Hormel canned hams as possible—all in one of those shining symbols of capitalism, the shopping cart.

Three couples, some married, some not, are introduced by host Bill Malone, a mild-mannered native of Brooklyn who broke into broadcasting covering athletics for his college radio station, an experience he undoubtedly tapped when describing the action on *Supermarket Sweep.* Malone starts off by producing several items of merchandise from the market, and the three ladies are asked to guess the value, which they ring up on their own cash registers. The winner in each case gets extra seconds tacked on to her "team's" allotted one-minute "sweep" of the store. This alone can be the determining factor in who the winner ultimately will be. At the sound of a loud bell, the sweep begins. The men take off like possessed robbers wheeling baskets through the aisles, stuffing them with turkeys, "imported" champagne, and other high-priced items available.

"It's hard to tell exactly what makes a good sweeper," said producer Allan Wallace in *TV Guide*. "It isn't just speed. We've had college track stars compete and some of them didn't do well at all because they tended to race around the store too fast without picking up enough items."

Since a five-item limit keeps contestants from stocking up on high-ticket merchandise like cartons of cigarettes, players spend a considerable amount of time at the meat counter. It's a sorry sight: three grown men grabbing wildly at rump roasts and Cornish game hens. The sweep continues as the roaring crowd of spectators counts down the few remaining seconds. Smiling grocery checkers tally up the "bills" with $250 an admirable total. (This was 1966, folks.) Winner takes all, literally.

"We just came here to have a good time," said one contestant, slapping some poultry. "Have you ever seen such a big turkey?"

RANDOM COMMENTS FROM CONTESTANTS

"This is a real good store with nice wide aisles."

"The turkeys are very good for sweeping. They're about thirteen dollars apiece. The hams may be a little small and the steaks are only fair, but the rib roasts are great. I did very well on those."

"You know, I've never really noticed how beautiful a supermarket could be!"

"Olive oil saved me once. But make sure to get the imported stuff."

"My family has been eating steak for breakfast, lunch, and dinner ever since we started."

David Susskind, Talent Associates, Ltd. president: "I care about TV, so I'm talking—the programing is lousy, stupid, and cowardly."

"You will enjoy shopping in our store specializing in efficient self-service," said Bill Malone, host of *Supermarket Sweep*.

SOME KIND WORDS FROM . . .

Variety:
"Daytime paean to human greed."

TV Guide:
"Shoplifting on a grand scale. . . ."

Harry Harris of the *Philadelphia Inquirer:*
"And I thought *Let's Make a Deal* was bad!"

THE BUSINESS BEHIND THE BOX

"I'd like our medium to be a more prideful place in which to work," said producer David Susskind, partner in Talent Associates, Ltd., a leading supplier of TV programs. "When intelligent people say that TV is no good, it hurts me." It doesn't hurt as much as it astounds us that Susskind, a respected entrepreneur of many fine TV programs, was actually associated with something as detestable as *Supermarket Sweep,* the shallowest of game shows. It started with an idea, considered a "natural" all along Madison Avenue's advertising row. A quickie pilot was shot, hauled over to ABC and promptly picked up. Previewed at test theaters, the show ran up the most enthusiastic response ratings ever assembled for a daytime offering. ABC hurriedly jettisoned a failing one-hour talk show starring Phyllis

Kirk and plopped *Supermarket Sweep* (and *The Dating Game*) in its place. Within a month of its premiere in December 1965, viewership had tripled to more than 2.5 million households. *Supermarket Sweep* continued to rack up impressive ratings, with a hefty $40,000-a-show budget, about $10,000 over the usual for a daytime game show.

Each week the *Sweep* crew pulled up to a different large, modern suburban supermarket, erected a bank of bleachers inside, and proceeded to convert the local market, as Peter Andrews wrote in *TV Guide*, "into a stage where the company can act out its own version of the American Dream." One week it was Levittown, New York, where Mrs. Harold Rathsan managed to corral thirty-five turkeys, twenty-two lawn chairs, hundreds of pounds of meat, canned goods, and a trip to the Bahamas. Another week it was the Food Fair in Livingston, New Jersey, or the Grand Union in Alexandria, Virginia.

By July 1967, *Sweep* had run its course, only to be resurrected a week later with a new title, *The Honeymoon Race*, wherein three newlywed couples competed for prizes in "a supermarket scavenger hunt" at the Hollywood Mall Shopping Center in Hollywood, Florida. It struggled through a single season before fading into oblivion, to the great Boot Hill of failed game shows that are best forgotten . . . except by TV historians like us.

THE SURVIVORS

THE GUILTY PARTIES

Creators:	Harold Robbins with Richard Deroy, John Wilder, Michael Gleason
Executive Producer:	Walter Doniger
Producers:	Richard Caffey, William Frye, Gordon Oliver
Associate Producers:	John Wilder, Michael Gleason
Directors:	Walter Doniger, John Newland, Michael Ritchie
Writers:	John Wilder, Michael Gleason, et al.
Cameraman:	William Margulies
Film Editor:	John Kaufman, Jr.
Sound:	Lyle Cain
Costumes by:	Luis Estevez, Nolan Miller
Music by:	Stanley Wilson

A Universal Television production in association with The Harold Robbins Company, Inc. for ABC-TV.

Starring Lana Turner as Tracy Carlyle Hastings, George Hamilton as Duncan Carlyle, Kevin McCarthy as Philip Hastings, Ralph Bellamy as Baylor Carlyle, Rossano Brazzi as Antaeus Riakos, Louis Hayward as Jonathan Carlyle, Diana Muldaur as Belle, Louise Sorel as Jean Vale, Michael Vincent as Jeffrey Hastings, Kathy Cannon as Sheila Riley, Robert Viharo as Miguel Santerra, Robert Lipton as Tom Steinberg, Pamela Tiffin as Rosemary Price; with Natalie Schafer, Clu Gulager, Celeste Yarnell, Bartlett Robinson, Jean-Paul Vignon, and Richard Eastman.

Debuted Monday, September 29, 1969, 9 P.M. E.D.T. on ABC-TV.

THE FORMAT

Webster's Dictionary defines soap opera as "a serial drama . . . characterized by stock domestic situations and often melodramatic or sentimental treatment." Despite all the insistence to the contrary by *The Survivors'* creators and producers, it is 99 44/100 percent pure soap opera: a *Peyton Place* of the veddy, veddy rich, and nothing like Britain's *Forsythe Saga* after which it was purportedly patterned. Here goes . . .

Duncan Carlyle (George Hamilton), the handsome playboy son of Baylor Carlyle (Ralph Bellamy), patriarch and president of The Carlyle Bank, one of the world's last private banking institutions, walks away from a Grand Prix race he was winning for a quick tryst with a chick in his private jet, but the aircraft is hijacked and flown to South America where a Simon Bolivar-ish buddy is waging a revolution that he wants the fabulously wealthy Carlyle Bank to finance. Meanwhile, back in the States, Duncan's half-sister, Tracy Carlyle Hastings (Lana Turner), is celebrating the twentieth anniversary of her loveless marriage to a snake-in-the-silken-sheets Philip Hastings (Kevin McCarthy) with a candlelit dinner at which it is revealed that she has suffered through the marriage for the sake of her teenage son Jeffrey (Michael Vincent, a/k/a Jan-Michael Vincent), whose sire is a man other than her husband. But at the bank, Papa Carlyle has discovered that his son-in-law, the aforementioned snake Hastings, after twenty years on the bank payroll, has bilked the kitty out of $675,000, and tells his secretary Belle (Diana Muldaur), whose services the old man enjoys both in and out of the office, to draw up a letter of resignation for Hastings. We also learn that Baylor had promised Philip the presidency of the bank when he married Tracy (she was three months pregnant at the time— "the family disgrace"), but now Baylor wants him out. But if Hastings is forced to resign, he'll tell the world about Jeff the bastard, which causes Tracy to suffer interminably. Meanwhile, Duncan arrives back in the United States to try to finance his friend's revolution but is mercilessly beaten up by some Latino bullies. . . .

And *The Survivors* saga continued . . . for some fifteen plodding chapters. If you have a strong constitution, we could go on with the story, which is next to unbelievable. On top of it all, it is endlessly moralizing—which, in a show as tasteless as this, is the last straw. As Cleveland Amory of *TV Guide* pointed out: "The idea of taking one's morals from Mr. Robbins is like taking higher economics from Bonnie and Clyde."

MEMORABLE MOMENTS

Tracy pleads with Philip to keep the illegitimacy of her son Jeffrey a secret. . . . Baylor visits Jeffrey's school, intending to tell the boy he is illegitimate. . . . Jeffrey becomes involved in a demonstration in school.... Baylor tells Belle that he hasn't long to live.... Jeffrey and Philip have a fiery confrontation.... Philip has a scheme in mind when he offers Tracy a divorce.... Jeff has a falling out with student radicals.... Tracy tells Jeff that Philip is not his father.... Baylor suspects Belle and Duncan are having an affair.... Sheila tries to stop Jeff from destroying the school computer.... Duncan discovers Baylor's dead body.... Baylor's will is read.... Philip plots anew to gain control of the bank.... Jeff learns that Riakos is his father [finally].

CLASSIC DIALOGUE

TRACY (*to her father*):   "We're your children, Baylor. You shaped and molded us. The fruit doesn't fall far from the tree."

DUNCAN (*to a South American dictator*):   "People who back revolutions don't advertise."

BAYLOR (*to Philip*):   "I've been to the horse's mouth. I'm not interested in the opinion of the other end."

DUNCAN (*to Belle on the occasion of Baylor's death*):   "I loved him. Even when I hated him, ... I loved him."

PHILIP (*to Tracy about their marriage*):   "Let's try to make it work. We've tried everything else."

DUNCAN (*to Baylor*):   "Keep refusing to deal with today's people and you'll be yesterday's!"

RIAKOS (*to Tracy*):   "Riakos was not good enough for the Carlyles, but his seed is!"

"I've never done TV before—except for a few guest appearances. I have a feeling it's going to be a grind, a lot of hard work. Oh, well, I'm committed. I'll either sink or swim," predicted *Survivors'* star Lana Turner.

"The role I played was nothing but a glossy image left over from my MGM days when I was always cast as a wealthy kid, part of the jet set. . . . We played *The Survivors* too straight, I think. We might have done better if we had camped it up," says George Hamilton.

The top-billed stars of *The Survivors*, Lana Turner and George Hamilton, played Tracy Carlyle Hastings and Duncan Carlyle, feuding progeny of Baylor Carlyle, played by Ralph Bellamy.

The *Survivors*, Version #1—set in Europe. The *Survivors*, Version #2—set in the U.S.A. Notice the difference: Lana's hairdo.

SOME KIND WORDS FROM . . .

Lawrence Laurent of the *Washington Post*:
"A star-packed hour of trashy troubles of the very rich. . . ."

Daily Variety:
"If these are the survivors, what were they like who didn't make it??"

Cecil Smith of the *Los Angeles Times*:
". . . there is not a character, a situation, or a line of dialogue that is remotely associated with human beings."

Entertainment World:
"High camp disaster. . . ."

Kevin McCarthy, who played Lana Turner's husband Philip, once appeared on Broadway in a play titled *The Survivors*. Ms. Turner starred in the movie version of *Peyton Place* to which her TV series was often likened.

FROM THE HORSE'S . . . (Harold Robbins)

Q: You originally saw *The Survivors* as an updated, Americanized *Forsythe Saga,* right?
A: It could have been. It was designed that way. I don't know what closed it off. I submitted a ten-page synopsis of *The Survivors* which sold to Universal in that form. Later I extended this into a lengthy treatment of which not one-tenth was used. I saw the final segment on TV, and my original idea had not progressed beyond page eight of my adaptation—that's the truth. As it turned out, it was their *Survivors,* not mine.

Q: Who are the so-called survivors?
A: There are two kinds. The original intent was to show the people who survive with the morality of today, who want to use their wealth to do good, to help build things, and there are other people and they survive very well, who say there *is* wealth but it is just for me.

Q: You were being handsomely paid for the use of your name, but how was the public to know what you wrote and what you didn't write?
A: Well, I didn't write any of that ridiculous crap about the South American revolution or Lana's goody-goody son getting busted in student demonstrations!

THE BUSINESS BEHIND THE BOX

"I want to reach a new audience with television," explained super-author Harold Robbins a month prior to the fall 1969 premiere of *The Survivors* on ABC. "The 30 million nonreaders. A writer doesn't write for the closet, you know." With twelve novels under his belt and some 50 million copies in print, Robbins decided to write a novel that would be visualized, not read. He got the idea for his "visual" novel in the early 1960s but didn't approach a network until 1964.

"I went to Jim Aubrey at CBS," Robbins acknowledged, "and I asked him for a minimum of a hundred hours on the air. I was considering writing *The Adventurers* for TV." CBS passed on the idea: too much money for a "story." Paramount and Joe Levine were bidding $1 million for the unwritten book which later became a film starring Ernest Borgnine and Candice Bergen. "But," the wealthy author continued, "the idea still intrigued me. I realized I couldn't get TV to the point where it would pay the same kind of money movies bring. So I got the idea of doing a novel *never* published, so that the basic economics would make this possible."

Over a casual lunch in New York with his lawyer Paul Gitlin, Robbins outlined the idea for *The Survivors,* an entire novel to stretch over two years, divided into one-hour installments. Unknown to his client, Gitlin hurried off to ABC headquarters and within hours, Robbins was offered the most lucrative writing assignment in TV history—one which could earn him $5.5 million for the right to air his still unwritten, barely titled TV series.

Robbins himself met with ABC corporate president Leonard Goldenson and outlined his idea. "What's it going to be?" the broadcasting executive queried Robbins. "We have to know what the story is about."

"I was curious myself," recalled Robbins. "I hadn't thought it through yet. I walked over to the window behind Goldenson's desk. I looked out the thirty-fifth floor, beyond Central Park, and could see the West Seventy-Ninth Street Boat Basin. There was a yacht moored in the Hudson. I started improvising: 'Here's your opening scene. The cameras focus on a yacht tied up off Manhattan. Then we zoom in on a bed in a stateroom. It's a big bed, in a big stateroom. The bed has black satin sheets. In the bed, there's a blonde. She's a gorgeous blonde. She's naked and . . .' "

"Stop! We'll buy it," the network guys said.

"There is this banking family," Robbins continued. "Morgan or Rothschild types, with the second generation vying among themselves for command after the death of the patriarch." *The Survivors* would be more sophisticated, Robbins promised, than conventional TV fare. "A story," he called it cleverly, "of today's morals. If people go to bed together, they'll go to bed together on the show. We are not bowing down to TV in any way."

ABC was sold with nary a script or pilot, something usually unheard of, and Universal was commissioned to produce it, although that would involve deficit financing of about $50,000 per show. Robbins, on the other hand, would get a percentage of any profits (seven European countries bought the show sight-unseen), plus $10,000 a show. Furthermore, he was guaranteed a full twenty-six weeks the first year, instead of the customary fifteen or seventeen, and payment for a second season of twenty-six shows whether it bombed or not. For that gilt-edged contract, Robbins gave ABC only a nine-page treatment. (Later, the novelist fleshed out the characters in a 100-page story "bible.")

In April 1968, ABC trumpeted the project, announcing that Lana Turner and George Hamilton had been signed for starring roles at salaries of $11,000 and $17,500 per week, respectively. *The Survivors* would premiere not that fall, but a year later, in 1969. It was a sure-fire hit, determined by these elements: Robbins; money—it would be about wealthy and powerful jet-setters, glamour, and foreign locales where almost all of it would be filmed; stars Turner, Hamilton, and Ralph Bellamy. Most important, it would inherit the time slot that launched the network's *Peyton Place* series a few seasons earlier.

Armed with Robbins' storyline, writers hired by Universal hacked out the actual scripts, known as "chapters." Producer William Frye was allocated the highest series budget in TV history, nearly $8 million for the first year. Some

$200,000 was spent on the set—four times the average—and another $100,000 on wardrobe, half of it for Miss Turner.

During the first week of shooting on the French Riviera, Lana Turner was involved in a verbal and physical hassle with producer Frye. She refused to wear paste jewelry. She couldn't get into the mood of her part, as a person of enormous wealth, unless she wore the real thing. Frye couldn't be bothered, he said, and got a slap across the face. He slapped back—on both cheeks—and she would not work again as long as he was producer. (A similar incident happened a few months later when it was learned that the budget for Lana's wardrobe had run out at about the halfway mark in the thirteen-week cycle of the series. The Universal "front office" contingent went down to the set to inform the aging movie queen of this budget setback. "That's all right," she answered calmly, "I'll just go home and when you get some more money, let me know.")

With Frye gone, Grant Tinker, Universal-TV vice president (and husband of Mary Tyler Moore), was dispatched to France to supervise production. He was replaced by Gordon Oliver who was replaced finally by Walter Doniger (*Maverick* and *Peyton Place*), who promptly wrote a forty-page, single-spaced critique of what was wrong with Robbins' outline and the scripts to date. Out went a dozen writers with their eight story outlines, three completed scripts and five more in the works.

Two production supervisors and a dozen writers later, after two months of shooting and $1 million in expenses, Universal still had to get its first usable episode. ABC was getting nervous. "We threw out the shows Harold worked on," explained an executive at the network. "The stuff dragged. He was explaining how a great banking institution really worked. But who cared about banks?" Just about the only remnants of Robbins' concept left were the characters' names (he got the Carlyle name because he stayed at the Carlyle Hotel in New York) and their relationships to each other.

.After the premiere on Monday, September 29, 1969, at 9 P.M. opposite an NBC network movie, CBS's *Mayberry, R.F.D.* and *The Doris Day Show*, Mason Williams, a writer for the Smothers Brothers, wrote and paid for an anonymous ad in the trade papers: "Congratulations to ABC-TV for coming up with the new series *The Survivors*, starring $8 million and no sense." This ilk of press incensed Miss Turner as did reviews which praised her costar Kevin McCarthy more than her. As panic set in, she ordered her Universal bosses to cut McCarthy's part severely in future episodes.

Fortunately, there were few future episodes. *The Survivors* was running third in the ratings to the opposition. For its debut show, it garnered a 20.5 rating with a 29 share; four weeks later, it had a 10.1 rating and a 15 share of the audience. By

Thanksgiving, just two months after the premiere, ABC issued the pink slip, acknowledging that *The Survivors* would be replaced in January by *Paris 7000* starring George Hamilton ("First they had the idea of continuing my *Survivors* character but I said no to that," said Hamilton).

Before the debut of *The Survivors*, a reporter for the *New York Times* had asked Robbins, "What is the story you have to tell?"

"It is that some people survive," the novelist explained, "and others don't."

And that some shows survive and others. . . .

S.W.A.T.

THE GUILTY PARTIES

Creator:	Robert Hamner
Executive Producers:	Aaron Spelling, Leonard Goldberg
Producers:	Rick Husky, Robert Hamner, Gene Levitt, Barry Shear
Directors:	Harry Falk, George McCowan, Earl Bellamy, Bruce Bilson, William Crane, Richard Benedict, et al.
Writers:	Fred Freiberger, Jack Fogarty, Herbert Bermann, Sean Baine, Ben Masselink, Walter Black, et al.
Cameraman:	Tim Southcott
Film Editors:	Leon Carrere, Clay Bartel
Music by:	Barry DeVorzon
Casting:	Claire Newell

A Spelling/Goldberg Production for ABC-TV.

Starring Steve Forrest as Lieutenant Dan "Hondo" Harrelson, Rod Perry as Sergeant David "Deacon" Kay, Robert Urich as Officer Jim Street, Mark Shera as Officer Dominic Luca, James Coleman as Officer T. J. McCabe, Ellen Weston as Betty Harrelson, Michael Harland as Matt Harrelson, and David Adams as Kevin Harrelson.

Debuted Monday, February 24, 1975, 9 P.M. E.S.T. on ABC-TV.

THE FORMAT

No doubt it happened: While all America was watching a southeast Los Angeles home being bombarded by countless rounds of gunfire and listening to newsmen speculating on whether or not a certain kidnapped newspaper heiress was in that unpretentious little wooden house or not, some little kid watching TV in wide-eyed amazement probably sputtered, "Wow! Just like on *S.W.A.T.!*"

That was May 17, 1975, less than three months after the premiere of *S.W.A.T.* on ABC-TV. S.W.A.T. stands for Special Weapons And Tactics, a special team of police officers operating in large cities like Los Angeles. Trained to take over when the "regular" police force is incapable of handling an emergency situation, S.W.A.T. on television represented something of a fraud. *Real* S.W.A.T. teams are rarely called upon, and when they are, a team is gathered for the occasion. (But since when does TV worry about realism?)

When the "hot line" rings, Lt. Dan "Hondo" Harrelson (Steve Forrest) answers the call, putting the gears of his S.W.A.T. team into motion. A Vietnam vet, Hondo oversees his quartet of henchmen—each a specialist in some sort of handiwork (sharpshooting, explosives, aerial rope athletics, etc.). Out rolls the specially equipped S.W.A.T. bullet-proof van and, in moments the team is at the scene of a major crime, bailing out like paratroopers, ready for action. Just what was it going to be this time? A suicidal maniac armed with a sawed-off shotgun? A Charles Manson-type barricaded behind the door of his house? A cat up a tree?

A member of Los Angeles' real S.W.A.T. team, *S.W.A.T.*'s technical advisor Rick Kelbaugh—on leave because of on-the-job injuries—tried his damnedest to inject realism into the show. But in order to have enough action in the hour segment of *S.W.A.T.*, writers conjured up more violence than a real S.W.A.T. team sees in an entire year! Kelbaugh says: "In the TV show, we may have four to six such incidents a night. It sometimes bothers me that our five guys look like supermen. In real life, there are not permanent S.W.A.T. teams, but only policemen on regular duty who take S.W.A.T. training courses and are subject to call-up only in emergencies. Also, in real life, the killing of a human being isn't taken lightly. We agonize over it in our hearts and minds, and we have to go through hours of intense interrogation to convince the department the killing was justified."

Aside from its cornucopia of violence, *S.W.A.T.*'s other main claim to fame was its extreme right-wing attitude—everything can be solved with a gun. The show brought to the home screen the enactment of a fantasy unfortunately shared by millions of Americans.

MEMORABLE MOMENTS

- A psychopathic Satanist, the leader of a coven dubbed the Butcher Brigade, swears vengeance on his prosecutors after a bloody escape from a hospital prison ward.

- To bait a trap for a sniper, Officer Jim Street dates a woman who lost three previous boyfriends to the killer.

- A middle-Eastern terrorist group takes a professional basketball team hostage to back its demands for money, a getaway plane and worldwide release of political prisoners.

- After a bullet creases his skull, Hondo is reluctant to accept the headaches, dizzy spells, and blurred vision he experiences as symptoms of serious injury.

SOME KIND WORDS FROM ...

Daily Variety:
"Elitist squad could have overtones of the SS as men whip around in their 'war wagon.' Undoubtedly, pasteboard characters will survive and thrive in cops-and-robbers climate without any concern for depth or performance."

People magazine:
"[*S.W.A.T.*] should stand for Simplistic, Warlike And Totalitarian."

Cleveland Amory of *TV Guide:*
"The premiere episode was offensive from every possible angle. . . .
Offense No. 2 was what might be called the underlying theme of *S.W.A.T.*—that the best way to beat crime is to beat people up. Offense No. 3—this is the idea that *S.W.A.T.* is the 'cream' of the force—that only they can do the job and that the ordinary police officer is no good. . . .
On top of all these offenses, the show is so predictable you can bet on it."

It's life in a "Pressure Cooker" in this episode of *S.W.A.T.*, telecast March 17, 1975, as Steve Forrest as Lt. Dan "Hondo" Harrelson leaps out of the S.W.A.T. van to save the world.

(*above*) The cast of *S.W.A.T.*: (*l. to r.*) Mark Shera as Dominic Luca, Robert Urich as Jim Street, Rod Perry as Sgt. David "Deacon" Kay, and James Coleman as T. J. McCabe. Steve Forrest (*extreme right*), as Lt. "Hondo" Harrelson, briefs his S.W.A.T. team. How to do in a grandmother intent on bombing the local Social Security office.

For nine years, TV viewers knew actor Steve Forrest as a villain and a creep. Finally, *S.W.A.T.* came along and Forrest got his wish—to play a good guy—a G.I. Joe with *real* bullets.

Ready for combat is "Hondo" Harrelson, S.W.A.T. commander. These bullhorns became a popular toy for kids bent on becoming S.W.A.T. members when they grew up. Golly gee!

Recognize him? That's Robert Urich, today's Dan Tanna of TV's *Vega$* show. Here he shows his prowess at lowering a gun down to a comrade. Note the scaffolding behind the ersatz building at the Twentieth-Century-Fox lot.

Steve Forrest posing alongside a dummy replica for the September 20, 1975, episode ("Kill S.W.A.T.") of *S.W.A.T.*

THE BUSINESS BEHIND THE BOX

In the spring of 1975, a few months after the debut on ABC of *S.W.A.T.*, the *New York Times* ran a piece on gang violence in that city. Members of a prominent street gang were asked to rate their favorite TV shows. Their number one choice was *S.W.A.T.* because "lots of cops get hurt."

   S.W.A.T. made television a prime purveyor of cold, calculated murder. "Cop shows" have always been a staple of the medium, dating back to *Dragnet* and even before the 1952 Jack Webb series moved from radio to TV. But until *S.W.A.T.* entered America's living rooms, police drama always reassured us by showing how capable our police are. Then Spelling/Goldberg, a TV production empire headed by former actor-writer Aaron Spelling and one-time ABC programing chieftain Leonard Goldberg, decided we needed a graphic cop show, a program that glorified a certain small aspect of normal police activities.

S.W.A.T. had its genesis as a 1974 special two-hour edition of ABC's *The Rookies* series. The venerable Top-Twenty show about the trials and tribulations of a bunch of young L.A. cops right out of the police academy, was also a Spelling/Goldberg production and one of the few hit series on the ABC network. Fred Pierce, president of the TV web—during pre-Fred Silverman days—was anxious to bolster his nighttime schedule and, with the help of Michael Eisner, the network's West Coast chief of program development, he bought six new series to use as midseason replacements, planning to put them on the air January 1975. Among them were *Baretta, Barney Miller,* and *S.W.A.T.*

Originally titled *S.W.A.T.T.* (Special Weapons And Tactical Team), the action series debuted Monday, February 24, 1975, in the nine-to-ten o'clock time slot, with an episode titled "The Killing Ground," an apt moniker. The show quickly gained not only recognition for being a weekly Armageddon on the home screen, but also racked up those Nielsen numbers like crazy. After just six episodes aired, *S.W.A.T.* rose to fourth place in the National Nielsens which meant 33 million Americans were watching the high-powered adventures of "Hondo" Harrelson and his force of militia men.

In Congress, House Communications Subcommittee chairman Torbert H. Macdonald (*D-Mass.*) singled out *S.W.A.T.* as a prime example of rampant and brutal violence portrayed on TV. "The bloodshed and killing in shows like *S.W.A.T.,*" he said, "is the worst thing to hit the United States since the plague."

The public outcry against violence finally ruled. *S.W.A.T.* episodes were toned down and the producers were proud to boast that in one such segment, absolutely *no one* was murdered; the S.W.A.T. team merely concentrated its efforts to save screaming senior citizens from burning up in a blazing nursing home. Producer Spelling, once a prolific TV writer (*Johnny Ringo, Honey West, Amos Burke,* et al.) and former partner of Danny Thomas (Thomas/Spelling Productions gave us *The Mod Squad*), went so far as to hire an old veteran, Rose Marie, to play Hilda the Sandwich Lady in hopes of having her spunky chit-chat show us that those S.W.A.T. guys are just like us—real people, just doin' their job.

Out with the blood-and-guts and in with true drama was the order of the day at ABC. Unfortunately for both the network and Spelling/Goldberg, this maneuver spelled the end of *S.W.A.T.* Viewers made it clear that the violence was what they wanted.

THE TAMMY GRIMES SHOW

THE GUILTY PARTIES

Creator:	George Axelrod
Executive Producer:	William Dozier
Producers:	Richard Whorf, Alex Gottlieb
Director:	Don Taylor
Writers:	Ralph Goodman, Roland Wolpert, et al.
Cameraman:	Ralph Woolsey
Film Editor:	Newell Kimlin
Music by:	Warren Barkis
Theme Song by:	Johnny Williams
Casting:	Mike McLean

A Twentieth Century-Fox TV production in association with Greenway Productions and Tamworth Productions for ABC-TV.

Starring Tammy Grimes as Tamantha (Tammy) Ward, Richard Sargent as Terence Ward, Hiram Sherman as Uncle Simon, and Maudie Prickett as Mrs. Ratchett, the housekeeper.

Debuted Thursday, September 8, 1966, 8:30 P.M. E.D.T. on ABC-TV.

THE FORMAT

Said Jack Gould in the *New York Times*: "Tammy Grimes enjoys a fragile talent that requires delicate handling and understanding." Pity Tammy Grimes, a truly talented stage actress with a unique personality, who was saddled with a disaster worse than the *Hindenburg*. As if lifted from a book of unused TV sitcom formats, her role as a "madcap heiress" was just too contrived. It might have been made palatable with some decent scripts, but the ones dished up for her were anything but helpful.

Tamantha Ward (God, what a name!) is employed as a PR officer in the Department of Human Relations of the Perpetual Bank of America where her twin brother Terence (Dick Sargent) is the eleventh vice president. The reason for the nepotism is simple enough: The president of the bank is tight-fisted Uncle Simon (Hiram Sherman). But wait, there's more. Tammy and Terence have coinherited the family fortune, but the controller of the pursestrings (the administrator of the trust) is none other than gruff old Uncle Simon who grimaces and bitches every time Tamantha asks for an advance on her sizable allowance. And with that premise, we now usher common sense, believability, and audience identification right out the door.

The show's scriptwriters obviously fell into that mid-1960s trap whereby to be a hit, a sitcom had to have a totally implausible gimmick like being a witch, monster, or cartooned superhero. Granted, a few clicked and clicked big, but many more failed. The main thrust of the cockeyed premise here is the fact that while Tamantha has no business sense whatsoever, Terence, the devout square, is a whiz in that department. Sexy, lovable, kooky (you can tell she's a kook by her funny voice), Tammy is always on the lookout for the "little people," throwing concern *and* money their way when necessary, which is most of the time.

Like subsequent scripts (only four shows aired), the first outing offered little character development, hardly any well-reasoned flow of events, and nothing in the way of comedy, slapstick or otherwise. Expendable as the plots may have been, the TV bigwigs saw them as merely the framework on which Miss Grimes was to weave her magic. Alas, even the most talented of performers cannot rise above a witless and mundane series like the one her writers dished up for her.

MEMORABLE MOMENTS

■ Tammy may have her chance to see the world—she's stuck on the ship that is taking her brother on a Naval Reserve tour.

■ Uncle Simon refuses to give Tammy $50,000 for her favorite charity, but he may have to ante up after all—kidnappers are demanding 50 G's for her return.

■ Tammy tries to help a friend by parlaying $20 and a one-way plane ticket to Las Vegas into $5,000.

■ To put a halt to Tammy's incessant clothes buying, Uncle Simon exiles her to Cobbs Corner, a town so rustic it doesn't have a dress shop.

Dick Sargent played Tammy's brother Terence. When the sitcom was axed, Sargent vowed: "I may starve, but I won't accept a series again playing a second lead. Life's too short to spend a career playing second fiddle." Three years later, he accepted producer Bill Asher's offer to replay Dick York as Elizabeth Montgomery's husband on *Bewitched*. Not only the second banana, but also the second actor to play the role.

The fourth and last episode of *The Tammy Grimes Show*, "Positively Made In Paris," had Miss Grimes posing as a French gendarme.

"Tammy has great warmth," remarked Richard Whorf, producer of the sitcom. "I know she'll appeal to the sophisticates. She has a pixie kookiness Lucille Ball doesn't have. The whole show rests on her. We don't know whether she will appeal to the flatlands, but I think they will adore her."

Broadway veteran Hiram Sherman played Uncle Simon, Tammy's favorite tightwad. The actor distinguished himself during TV's early years by appearing on *Studio One*, *Philco Theatre*, and *Hallmark Hall of Fame*. His studio biography, however, made special mention of the fact that since he sunburns easily, he has to avoid outdoor activities.

ABC promoted its three female comedy stars with a spoof of the old *Playhouse 90* title. Marlo Thomas had a five-year run with *That Girl* and Elizabeth Montgomery played the *Bewitched* witch for eight seasons—a role first offered to Tammy Grimes who lasted four weeks on her own show.

SOME KIND WORDS FROM . . .

Harry Harris of the *Philadelphia Inquirer:*
"Plotting for morons by morons. . . ."

Anthony LaCamera of the *Boston Record-American:*
"Who put the whammy on Tammy?"

Jack Gould of the *New York Times:*
". . . an ordeal."

Tammy Grimes following the quick demise of her show: "You know that you're not creating great art, so you let little things slip and pretty soon you've got a disaster."

FROM THE HORSE'S ... (Tammy Grimes)

Q: What do you feel was the main problem confronting your show?

A: George Axelrod wrote a wonderful pilot script that was really *me*. I mean it was a character that had some special parts of my personality. The other scripts after that just weren't the same. They tried to fit me into some kind of formula. I felt immediately that they weren't right. ... We had problems with each of them.

Q: Why then did you continue working on the show, knowing the results were inferior?

A: Well, you keep telling yourself, "It *couldn't* be as bad as I think it is." The pressure in front of the camera is tremendous. I blame myself for not trusting my instincts to stop the proceedings and yell: "Wait a minute! This thing has my name on it!" But I kept on letting things go, hoping they wouldn't show.

Q: Do you have any final thoughts?

A: I was asked to do the series because of my personality. You cannot blame anyone for it. Please don't blame anybody.

THE BUSINESS BEHIND THE BOX

On November 3, 1960, a star was born: Tammy Grimes opened on Broadway in Meredith Willson's *The Unsinkable Molly Brown*. That spring she trotted off with all the major acting plaudits, including the coveted Tony. Critics called her everything from a "sexy little screwball" to "an unkempt poodle," but most agreed with columnist Earl Wilson: "Tammy Grimes is a great big hit!"

The soap opera-ish saga of Tammy's bout with television began during the run of *Molly Brown*. Bill Dozier, then vice president in charge of West Coast operations for Screen Gems, the TV production arm of Columbia Pictures, tried to persuade Miss Grimes to accept the lead role in a new sitcom being developed by Sol Saks, a sort of twist on *I Married a Witch*. Tammy passed on the offer; she couldn't see herself as a witch, and didn't think the show would play well. Elizabeth Montgomery, on the other hand, *could* see herself as a witch, and *Bewitched* played for eight seasons.

Shortly thereafter, Dozier moved to Twentieth Century-Fox as an independent TV producer (Greenway Productions) where he put together the successful *Batman*, a surprise 1966 hit for ABC. Dozier kept thinking about a TV vehicle for Tammy whom he was certain could be "another Lucy," given the right format. Meanwhile—back in New York—Charles "Bud" Barry, senior vice president of TV/radio for the Young & Rubicam ad agency, was having similar notions about Miss Grimes. He thought Tammy was "magic" in *Molly Brown*, and he figured some of that magic could be put to work selling products on TV for General Foods, one of his agency's clients.

Dozier approached playwright George Axelrod, author of *The Seven Year Itch* and *Will Success Spoil Rock Hunter?*, both stage smashes, hoping the wizard could work his writing magic on Tammy. Axelrod huddled—as they say in the business—with Tammy, then went off to his typewriter and came up with *My Twin Sister,* a series about a pair of heiresses, one "madcap," one "square"—both roles to be played by Miss Grimes. Tammy liked the format all right, gave the green light to her friend and mentor Dozier, and in June 1965, everyone assembled on a soundstage at Twentieth Century-Fox to make a pilot with General Foods' money. A week before the cameras were set to grind, Axelrod changed his mind, making Tammy's twin sister a twin brother, Terence. Dozier quickly cast Dick Sargent, late of *One Happy Family* (which lasted half a season) and *Broadside* (it limped through a single semester), to play the fraternal twin.

The pilot, which had seven minutes of plotting (to use the word loosely)—the rest being a series of vignettes about the star—was glommed by everyone, including General Foods bigwigs who summarily walked out before the screening was over, asking to be dealt out (later to be replaced by Bristol-Myers).

The series went into production on June 20, 1966, and after this and three other episodes were completed, all the heavy artillery men assembled in a screening room to unveil the results. Two hours later, the lights came on and there was silence.

"We're sunk," someone from Bristol-Myers noted.

"It's not just a *bad* show," an ABC official added, "it's an unfixable show."

Expected disaster notwithstanding, ABC went full speed ahead with its fall promotion, one line of which promised that Tamantha would get into "extraordinarily funny situations which are excruciatingly painful to her sober-sided twin brother, Terence."

Old Terence wasn't the only one in pain. The series premiered Thursday, September 8, 1966, and it became crystal clear instantly that viewers by the millions preferred *My Three Sons* on CBS and the new *Star Trek* on NBC. It didn't take an ABC programing genius to figure out it had a flop of the first magnitude on its hands. The real problem was what to do and when. Ten episodes were already in the can and ABC had made a seventeen-episode commitment with Dozier. Chevrolet, sponsor of the hit *Bewitched,* was on ABC's back, claiming with good reason that *Tammy* wasn't their idea of a strong lead-in. So, on the morning of September 26, 1966, the same day as the series was set to resume production after a short hiatus, ABC canceled *The Tammy Grimes Show.*

Whom to blame? Surely "script trouble," a common ailment, was one consideration. One higher-up said that the masses couldn't understand Tammy's "peculiar speech patterns" (that sure didn't hurt Desi Arnaz). Bill Dozier had this to offer: "If it's a bomb, you fold up your tent and steal away." And Tammy Grimes said: "It was a shock. I kind of walked on the beach and tried to figure things out."

On cancellation day, coproducer Richard Whorf checked into St. Johns Hospital in Santa Monica with bleeding ulcers, and his comrade Gottlieb, before cleaning out his desk, sent Dozier three bottles of champagne and a card saying, "Who said she was unsinkable?"

THREE'S COMPANY

THE GUILTY PARTIES

Creators:	John Mortimer, Brian Cooke
	(based on their Thames-TV show,
	Man About the House)
Developed by:	Don Nicholl, Michael Ross, Bernie West
Producers:	Don Nicholl, Michael Ross, Bernie West
Production Executives:	Ted Bergmann, Don Taffner
Associate Producer:	Mimi Seawell
Directors:	Dave Powers, Bill Hobin
Writers:	Gary Belkin, George Burditt,
	Paul Wayne, Dixie Brown Grossman,
	Phil Hahn, Bryan K. Joseph,
	Dennis Koenig, Alan J. Levitt,
	Mike Marmer, et al.
Theme Music by:	Joe Raposo, Don Nicholl
Casting:	David Graham

An NRW Company production in association with TTC Productions, Inc. for ABC-TV.

Starring John Ritter as Jack Tripper, Joyce DeWitt as Janet Wood, Suzanne Somers as Chrissy Snow, Audra Lindley as Helen Roper, Norman Fell as Stanley Roper, and Richard Kline as Larry.

Debuted Tuesday, March 15, 1977, 9:30 P.M. E.S.T. on ABC-TV.

THE FORMAT

Janet Wood (Joyce DeWitt) and Chrissy Snow (Suzanne Somers) live in a well-kept Spanish-style apartment complex in Santa Monica, California, near the Pacific Ocean. Janet works in a florist shop and has a tongue about as sharp as the thorns on the roses she occasionally has to clip. Her roommate Chrissy is a stupid, blonde, sexpot typist, and the daughter of a puritanical minister.

One night, after a wild going-away party for their pregnant ex-roommate, the girls discover a passed-out person in their bathtub. The handsome leftover turns out to be a young gourmet cooking student named Jack Tripper (John Ritter). Perfect timing, for the girls were having an impossible time trying to keep up with the rent payments and had decided to begin looking for a new roommate. They ask Jack if he would like to move in—lock, stockpots and pans. He accepts and the spare room is no longer spare.

The main obstacle preventing the threesome from a trouble-free existence is the grumpy landlord, Stanley Roper (Norman Fell), who lives in the flat directly below them with his oversexed wife Helen (Audra Lindley). The prudish Mr. Roper is not about to allow a virile young stud like Jack to shack up with two gorgeous gals.

In order to keep the living arrangement intact, and to please Roper, Jack lets on that he's not the least bit interested in the girls—*any* girls for that matter. Consequently, whenever Roper is present, Jack has to act effeminate or face eviction. Mrs. Roper knows all about the scheme and is constantly providing a healthy share of lascivious leers, suspecting all-night orgies and the like, even though the relationships are said to be strictly platonic, much to Jack's chagrin.

Mrs. Roper's uncommon interest in the trio's sex lives is due to the fact that she has none of her own. Stanley's indifference toward her is the show's running gag, with randy Helen never missing an opportunity to belittle and humiliate hubby with her acid tongue. (No wonder he's impotent.) Given any situation, Mrs. Roper can find a way to twist it against Stanley: He's fixing the plumbing and says he hasn't got "the right equipment." Mrs. Roper retorts: "You're telling me."

From the opening sequence, showing Jack falling off his bicycle at the sight of a pair of shapely female buns, *Three's Company* manages consistently to deal with sex at the junior high school level.

MEMORABLE MOMENTS

- Janet contemplates silicone transplants after her boss promotes a voluptuous new employee to manager of the flower shop.

- In the girls' absence, Jack tosses a wild party and awakens the next day to find himself with an unlikely bedfellow, Mr. Roper.

- In the wee hours of the morning, a teary-eyed Chrissy comes home from a cheap bar with a sad tale of having been mistaken for a prostitute.

- Jack's friend borrows Chrissy's new movie projector for what he hopes will be a private screening of a pornographic movie.

- Janet and Chrissy are visited by a girl who says she's looking for Jack because he has gotten her in trouble.

CLASSIC DIALOGUE

MRS. ROPER: "Fix the doorbell, Stanley. It's time somebody's chimes were rung in this house."

JACK (*regarding Janet's having her breasts enlarged*): "You're making mountains out of molehills."

MR. ROPER (*looking at old golf scorecard*): "I really used to score pretty good in those days."
MRS. ROPER: "Times change."
MR. ROPER: "Maybe I need a better course to play on."

MR. ROPER (*commenting on noise from adjacent apartment*): "There goes that banging again."
MRS. ROPER: "Oh, c'mon. A little of that never hurt anybody."

Jack (John Ritter) and Janet (Joyce DeWitt) greet Chrissy (Suzanne Somers) with mixed emotions when she tells them that her father, a minister, is coming to visit their little den of iniquity.

SOME KIND WORDS FROM ...

Lee Margulies of the *Los Angeles Times:*
"... **inane, cheap sexual humor which is about as subtle as a mugging, and about as funny.**"

Aljean Harmetz of *TV Guide:*
"... **thigh-deep in double entendres. Nearly every scene ... pulls an undertow of smutty giggles with dialogue that is ... as sophisticated as the jokes generations of high school students have tried to get away with.**"

The *Hollywood Reporter:*
"... **marshmallow fluff and terribly coy.**"

Norman Fell, Suzanne Somers, Audra Lindley, Joyce DeWitt, and John Ritter, stars of one of the highest-rated sitcoms of the seventies—the brainless *Three's Company.*

In the episode "Larry's Bride," Stanley Roper tries to save money by providing the wedding music. The series likewise hit a sour note with most critics.

Jack and Chrissy enjoy some juicy entries in "Love Diary." John Ritter's father was Tex Ritter, the singing cowboy. Somers's main claim to fame was her brief but apparently memorable scene in *American Graffiti* where, as the beautiful blond in the T-Bird, she mouthed the words "I love you" to Richard Dreyfuss.

Every week 55 million viewers tune in. Here, Jack Tripper shows off his cupcakes. Viewers are waiting for the girls to show off theirs.

THE BUSINESS BEHIND THE BOX

Like *All in the Family* and *Sanford and Son* before it, *Three's Company* was based on a hit British TV series, a light concoction by writers John Mortimer and Brian Cooke called *Man About the House.* The idea about a pair of liberated females and one guy living under the same roof found its merry way across the Atlantic and onto the desk of Fred Silverman, ABC's resident programing genius, who loved the idea and ordered a pilot.

Silverman, who was Mike Dann's successor as head of programing at CBS and responsible for numerous hit shows like *Kojak, Cannon, Maude, Rhoda, The Waltons,* etc., defected to ABC in the spring of 1975 (a limousine and an unlimited expense account did the trick). By the winter of 1976, ABC was beginning to enjoy its first run of luck in years—*Happy Days, Donny and Marie, The Bionic Woman, Charlie's Angels,* and *Laverne and Shirley* were riding high in the ratings, assuring the network of many additional millions in advertising revenue.

With some extra programing coin to kick around, the pilot for *Three's Company* was put into production in 1976 with high hopes that it would find a berth in ABC's fall lineup. The sample film depicted the adventures of two budding *actresses* and the young stud *filmmaker* who is their roommate. Silverman saw the results and flashed a cold shoulder. It wasn't what he expected, so he decided to give it a second chance. He called in the triumvirate of Don Nicholl, Michael Ross, and Bernie West, some former CBS colleagues who had written many of the early *All in the Family* scripts and were producing *The Jeffersons* at the time. Their assignment was to produce a *new* version of *Three's Company*, one a little closer to the British model, *Man About the House.*

Don Nicholl recalls: "Silverman instructed us to make it the same kind of breakthrough in sexiness that *All in the Family* was to bigotry."

The three writer-producers rewrote the pilot, making the girls part of the "working class"—one a florist shop clerk, the other a typist—and the boy a cooking-school student. They recast one of the leads (Joyce DeWitt was not in the first version), filmed it before a live studio audience, and delivered the results to Silverman at ABC.

John Ritter, who plays the cooking-school student, Jack Tripper, remembers: "We were up for the fall [1976] schedule. We had been told that ABC would put on six new sitcoms, and we were number five. After I bought the champagne, they said it would be only four shows and we were still number five." *Three's Company* never made it on the air that September, but *Mr. T and Tina, Holmes and YoYo,* Nancy Walker, and Tony Randall did (only Randall lasted beyond the first thirteen weeks).

Silverman opted not to bury the pilot, but to put it in a holding pattern, hoping to throw it on the air the following spring. However, instead of simply airing the pilot to recoup some of ABC's investment, Silverman ordered five more episodes from Nicholl-Ross-West, planning to give it a "tryout." If the series did well enough, ABC would put it on the air come fall.

Not only did *Three's Company* do well, it did fantastically well. For its short six-week run, it racked up ratings sizeable enough to place it in the 11 position on Nielsen's 1976–77 *season* list—an unheard of feat.

Today, the show is seen in more than 22.5 million homes every week—translated, that means 55 million fans. It consistently rates in the Top Five programs, and is often in the number one spot.

"I'm helping to make America laugh!" Joyce DeWitt claims. "There's a lot of physical comedy in *Three's Company* and I don't begin to say we're as good as Chaplin and some of his contemporaries, but we *are* in that tradition."

The Little Tramp must be turning over in his grave.

TURN ON

THE GUILTY PARTIES

Creators:	George Schlatter, Digby Wolfe
Executive Producer:	George Schlatter
Producer:	Digby Wolfe
Director:	Mark Warren
Writers:	Leo Pine, Bob Arbogast, Albert Brooks, George Burditt, Ed Hider, Bryan Joseph, Jack Kaplan, Steve Pritzger, Norman Hudis
Director of Photography:	Guy Adenis
Cameraman:	Ross Kelsay
Electronic Music by:	Heller-Hamilton, Inc.
Animation by:	Mel Henke, Bill Melendez Productions

A Schlatter-Friendly Production for ABC-TV.

Featuring Bob Staats, Maura McGiveney, Bonnie Boland, Hamilton Camp, Teresa Graves, Maxine Greene, Ken Greenwald, Carlos Manteca, Chuck McCann, Cecile Ozorio, Mel Stewart, Alma Murphy, with guest star Tim Conway.

Debuted Wednesday, February 5, 1969, 8:30 P.M. E.S.T. on ABC-TV.

THE FORMAT

Two computer operators, one white and one black, sit with their backs to the camera facing a madly flashing IBM 360, or something. Says black to white, "I've never programed a program before." Neither had ABC, the network that chose to air this turkey as one of its "second season" shows on February 5, 1969.

Described as "a satire on our dehumanized society," *Turn On* was a "sensory assault involving . . . animation, videotape, stop-action film, electronic distortion, computer graphics—even people," according to its producer, one-time *That Was the Week That Was* writer Digby Wolfe. The multi-media barrage careened along for thirty minutes, sometimes with the screen split four ways, reaching for a dizzying 300 laughs, most of them poking supposed fun at contraception and homosexuality.

"All I can remember," one irate viewer wrote *TV Guide,* "is the word 'sex,' in huge letters, pounding across the screen." It was *Turn On*'s most sustained sequence, running several minutes. "Sex," its letters changing colors and emphasis—"Sex!", "Sex?", etc.—flashing mindlessly on center screen while the faces of guest host Tim Conway and *Turn On* regular Bonnie Boland flitted in and out of the picture, mugging suggestively at each other, to the tune of throbbing electronic sounds.

One-line gags, towed across the screen by animated airplanes, strained to be funny: "God Save the Queens," "Free Oscar Wilde," "Make Love Not Wine," "Israel Uber Alles," and "The Amsterdam Levee Is a Dike." To add to the mess, the show's sole set was a totally colorless plaster cyclorama and the cast wore "invisible" white booties. Therefore, everything seemed to be floating in a never-never land. *Time* magazine commented, "It all seemed to come from beautiful downtown nowhere."

Production credits would periodically turn up. Stretched out, this alone could have consumed the half-hour, and perhaps been a better show. But the computer/host made one large mistake: It folded, mutilated, bent, and spindled some of the most promising talent in the business.

Chuck McCann clowns for the camera.

Robert Culp and his wife France Nuyen were scheduled to guest host the second *Turn On* show, but it never aired.

One of the dozen or so *Turn On* crazies, Bonnie Boland. Several years later, she was featured on *Chico and the Man* as the "mailperson."

Tim Conway, who starred in his own share of flop shows, had the dubious distinction of hosting the first and last *Turn On.*

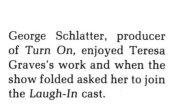

George Schlatter, producer of *Turn On,* enjoyed Teresa Graves's work and when the show folded asked her to join the *Laugh-In* cast.

FROM THE HORSE'S . . . (George Schlatter)

Q: *Turn On* was canceled the same night it premiered on ABC. Why?
A: I don't know why, but the network replaced us with old movies that showed violence, brutality, wife-swapping, and killing, in addition to the use of language not permitted in most homes.

Q: What was your purpose in doing such a show?
A: From the beginning, we said that the show would try new things, new forms, new styles, and take a more adult approach to humor. We spent a year developing the concept.

Q: In your estimation, why did the show fail?
A: We didn't do the show for the network or station managers, but for the public, which has always been eons ahead of what TV gives it. If ABC was right, that *Turn On* was just too much, then I look forward to a triumphant return of *My Mother, the Car.*

THE BUSINESS BEHIND THE BOX

Few television shows ever achieve distinction. Of the more than 2,500 or so programs that have come and gone since 1946, how many can you recall with some reverence? *I Love Lucy?* Uncle Miltie? *All in the Family,* certainly, and *Perry Mason, Studio One, The Mary Tyler Moore Show.* The moon landing in 1969 surely was a TV milestone. So was another 1969 television event: *Turn On.* Its fame, however, is of a different ilk. The series played one night and was canceled.

It happened like this. In the spring of 1968, the advertising boss of Bristol-Myers, Marvin Koslow, approached George Schlatter and Ed Friendly, packagers of NBC's phenomenon, *Laugh-In,* then TV's most popular program, and asked them to try to come up with a new half-hour series—"something unusual and provocative." As it turned out, *Turn On* had been kicking around as a concept predating *Laugh-In.* It *was,* in fact, closer to the original *Laugh-In* approach (Dan Rowan and Dick Martin did not figure in the early discussions for *Laugh-In*).

A *Turn On* pilot was shot and Koslow and his ad agency, Young & Rubicam, started shopping around the networks for a decent time slot. Both CBS and NBC turned thumbs down. "It was not any good," said an NBC programer. "It wasn't funny, and in many areas, it was in bad taste." CBS likewise questioned the content: "We said no, thank you. Not so much because the show was dirty but because there was not a joke in it. Also, it was so fast with the cuts and chops that some of our people actually got physically disturbed by it!"

A second pilot—somewhat less frenetic and dirty—was put together, and that's when ABC got interested. The network's Leonard Goldberg, vice president in charge of programing, claims: "We were striving for something different. We were seeking a completely new form for TV."

A major search for new talent convened when ABC signed Schlatter-Friendly to a firm eighteen-show contract, preparing to premiere *Turn On* "sometime early in 1969," as part of its "second season" programing assault. Schlatter and his producer Digby Wolfe coraled a dozen promising performers to headline the half-hour psychedelic satire. A few had prior TV experience, like Hamilton Camp who delighted viewers and critics with his performance as Andrew the handyman on *He and She.* Chuck McCann, a comedian with extensive credits as a New York TV kids' show host, was tapped for a regular spot. Fifteen cinema students from USC and UCLA, six graphic artists new to film and TV, two electronics students specializing in designing and developing equipment were given an opportunity to pool their creative resources to produce *Turn On.*

The two *Turn On* pilots were shown to the 200-odd ABC affiliates in October 1968 via closed-circuit screenings. Everyone agreed that Schlatter-Friendly had concocted the second coming of *Laugh-In,* and the network was panting to have one of its shows in the Top Ten.

Then February 5 rolled around. *Turn On* came on at 8:30 P.M. and went off—literally and completely—at 9 P.M., never to be seen or heard from again. As a spinoff, *Turn On* was nothing more than a simple-minded distillation of the dregs of *Laugh-In,* but without the latter's stars and company of players, but gutted by its dirtier intents. In plainer terms, it didn't belong on television.

The nation rose up in arms. Don Perris, general manager of WEWS in Cleveland, wired ABC-TV president Elton Rule (himself once a station manager): "If your naughty little boys have to write dirty words on the walls, please don't use *our* walls." WEWS, Perris promised, would carry no more of *Turn On.* Two days after the premiere no less than seventy-five stations, representing almost half the ABC lineup for the show, had said no to *Turn On.* In city after city, viewer dissent ran high: Three to one against the show was the norm.

Len Goldberg of ABC said: "The critics blasted the show. And we heard from the stations *loud* and clear. They felt it was not the kind of show we should have on our network. But most importantly, we heard from the viewers. The response was overwhelmingly negative. There really wasn't any decision for us to make—the feeling was unanimous."

On Monday, February 10, 1969—five days following the premiere/execution, the *Hollywood Reporter* ran a Page One headline that read: "ABC Turns Off 'Turn On,' " with the subheading "What Was Thought to Be a Series Turns Out to Be a Special—One-Time Only."

Schlatter-Friendly was upset with ABC's hasty decision to "pull" the show. "The dismissal of fifty bright people with something to say and with technical knowledge to execute their ideas because an ABC affiliate in Cleveland got a few calls from a handful of old ladies was tragic!" George Schlatter commented.

Let's hear it for the little old ladies of Cleveland!

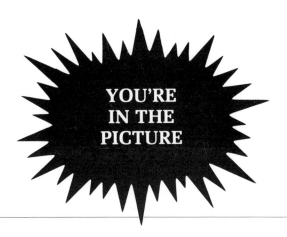

YOU'RE IN THE PICTURE

THE GUILTY PARTIES

Creators:	Bob Synes, Don Lipp
Producer:	Stephen R. Carlin
Director:	Seymour Robbie
Musical Director:	Norman Leyden
Sponsors:	Kellogg's, L&M cigarettes

A Stephen R. Carlin production in association with Jackie Gleason for CBS-TV.

Starring Jackie Gleason as host.

Debuted Friday, January 20, 1961, 9:30 P.M. E.S.T. on CBS-TV.

THE FORMAT

Realizing that the public has a very short memory and to keep his face out front, Jackie Gleason agreed to host the game show, *You're In the Picture*. As *Newsweek* pointed out, "The idea was disarmingly simple: a half-hour show in which four panelists would stick their heads through portholes cut in special plywood walls. The walls would depict things like *Alice in Wonderland* characters or high hurdle runners, and the panelists, unable to see the pictures, would try to guess the situation they were in." Sounds simple enough, and that was precisely the problem—it was *too* simple.

This meager premise left the herculean task of wringing entertainment out of the flimsy excuse for a game show up to the four guest players, and if they couldn't deliver the goods, the rest fell on Gleason's rounded shoulders. What the show was envisioned to be was this sprightly, casual question-and-answer tug-of-war between Gleason and his chatty foursome. In other words, a sophisticated parlor game for national television. This, of course, left no room for error and the unexpected (it was done live), and so Murphy's Law prevailed.

The panelists for the first (and last) installment were Jan Sterling, Pat Carroll, Pat Harrington, Jr., and Arthur Treacher. They managed to guess correctly two out of the five presented pictures, but it didn't really matter—the charity organization, CARE, benefited by being on the receiving end of 100 gift packages. This stipulation had a strange effect on the proceedings. While it did cancel out any possible avaricious competition, it also provided the panelists with little incentive. Critics saw through the charades, like a *Hollywood Reporter* writer who commented, "Major flaw—the participants don't take it seriously, so why should the audience?"

How could a director jazz up a show where nothing moves? Gleason, all 245 pounds of him, sat there practically motionless while the panelists were held prisoner in the plywood murals, like some sort of Colonial-day rascal in gallows (Pat Carroll got her head stuck in the cut-out during the rehearsal). Director Seymour Robbie could do nothing more than switch back and forth between cameras, which gave the show a terribly static appearance, quite the contrast to typical TV fare where the rule is, the faster the better.

On January 20, 1961, CBS and Jackie Gleason had given birth to a "stillborn" bore, and *You're In the Picture* never again showed its flopping face.

"The Great One," Jackie Gleason, wasn't so terrific on this turkey. He was so embarrassed by the debacle, he spent thirty minutes on TV apologizing for it.

Jan Sterling, roped into being one of the panelists on Jackie Gleason's wonderfully horrible quiz show, *You're In the Picture*. Losing the Oscar for *The High and the Mighty* wasn't enough.

SOME KIND WORDS FROM ...

Daily Variety:
"It is depressing to see a comic talent of Jackie Gleason's caliber wasting itself on such a limp, inane game."

Newsweek:
"This is a panel show??"

TV Guide:
"The biggest disaster since the Johnstown Flood."

Jackie Gleason:
"It made the H-bomb look like a two-inch salute!"

Arthur Treacher was popular for his droll-witted butler characters in early movies with Shirley Temple, and later gained a reputation as Merv Griffin's co-host. Picture him standing with his head through a hole-in-the-wall for a half-hour.

Noting that "honesty is the best policy," Gleason admitted his game show
was "a bomb." Nobody's perfect,
Jackie.

THE BUSINESS BEHIND THE BOX

Jackie Gleason's TV career began in 1949 with *The Life of Riley* which lasted only
six months (William Bendix successfully resurrected the role of Chester A. Riley
in 1953). In 1950, he was heading his own variety show on the DuMont network.
This hour-long outing established him as a true talent, as he breathed life into such
characters as Joe the Bartender, The Poor Soul, Reginald Van Gleason, etc. *The
Honeymooners,* that venerable never-say-die classic, got its start as a weekly
sketch, but in 1955 it broke off on its own as a CBS sitcom which ran only a year.
(The same thirty-nine episodes are shown over and over again today with respectable ratings in many major cities.) By the fall of 1956, Gleason was back
fronting a variety show, the format he worked best in and loved, but this time via
CBS.

   Which brings us to *You're In the Picture,* the 1961 game show. Although seen
on reruns of his variety show, Gleason had been conspicuously absent from the
tube for nearly two years—though he did occasionally substitute for Red Skelton
when the latter was too ill to perform on his own CBS show. By the end of 1960,
Gleason was itching to do something—almost anything so long as it wasn't as gru-
eling as the weekly variety show. Groucho Marx was hosting a super-successful
quizzer, *You Bet Your Life* which was nothing more than a simple question-and-
answer game built around Groucho's peerless ability to trade quips with wacky
contestants. If Marx could manage it, Gleason probably reasoned, so could he.

   Early in December 1960, Gleason was approached by the creators of *You're In
the Picture,* and "The Great One" fell for the show hook, line, and sinker—so much

so that he bought into it. CBS, anxious to have Gleason back on the tube, canceled *Mr. Garlund,* a dismal half-hour adventure series and turned over its Friday-at-9:30 slot to him.

Before the ink dried on the contracts, there was trouble. Many celebrities, because of previous commitments, declined invitations to appear on the show. It was only at the very last moment that Jackie himself managed to corral his first four guinea pigs for the premiere outing, scheduled for January 20, 1961. Lovely Jan Sterling (nominated as "Best Supporting Actress" for her role in *The High and the Mighty*) was flown in from California, but the time difference left her visibly weary. Pat Harrington, Jr., of the *Danny Thomas Show,* was rushed to New York to take Keenan Wynn's place, the latter having collided with a plate glass door less than twenty-four hours before showtime. His swollen snout was deemed unacceptable for closeups (perhaps his nose smelled trouble in the offing). Working under the gun, Gleason hardly had time for one last "And awaaaaay we go!" before the clock struck 9:30 P.M., and "Live from New York, it's *You're In the Picture* with your host Jackie Gleason!"

To Frank Leyden's orchestrated accompaniment, Gleason strolled onstage and introduced his guests. The rules were explained, then the travesty-to-come paused long enough for L&M and Kellogg's to get their words in edgewise. When the red lights on the TV cameras went out after the half-hour was over, Gleason knew he had laid one of the biggest eggs in show biz history and there was only one thing to do—apologize.

Same time, same station on the following Friday night, there appeared on the screen no *You're In the Picture* logo. Instead, viewers found a bare stage. The rotund comedian found his way to a spartan wooden chair and began to explain. Starting off with reminiscences about past failures, Gleason defended his critics: "You don't have to be Alexander Graham Bell to pick up the phone and find it's dead." This thirty-minute rap session with his loyal viewership endeared Jackie to millions.

The *Hollywood Reporter* noted, "Perhaps some of Gleason's gags were prepared, but most of what he said was off-the-cuff and from the heart—and he was never more witty, warm, friendly, and charmingly disarming than with his unforced, 'fireside' chat regarding his problem of what to do with a bad show—fix it or scrap it."

The following week, Gleason returned with a "talk" show, interviewing the likes of Mickey Rooney and Floyd Patterson. In a few weeks, however, Kellogg's pulled out of its contract, claiming that a talk show was not what they had ordered (could they have possibly preferred the clinker?). As Gleason pointed out during that last show: "Show business is a strange and intangible endeavor."

You're In the Picture—how sweet it wasn't.

INDEX

Page numbers in boldface indicate photographs

DUTTON PAPERBACKS OF RELATED INTEREST

POPULAR CULTURE

The TV Addict's Handbook, Bart Andrews
Automerica, Ant Farm
The Matineee Idols, David Carroll
The Book of Conquests, Jim Fitzpatrick
S.T.P., Robert Greenfield
Los Angeles, John Halpern
Fun House Five-and-Dime Memory Bank, Robert Heide and John Gilman ·
Wasn't the Future Wonderful?, Tim Onosko
The Incomplete Book of Failures, Stephen Pile
The Fantasy Almanac, Jeff Rovin
The Verse by the Side of the Road, Frank Rowsome, Jr.
Aphrodisia, Gary Selden
Pinball!, Roger Sharpe
Superstars, Alexander Walker
No Commercial Potential, David Walley

FILM

Nonfiction Film, Richard Meran Barsam
Nonfiction Film Theory and Criticism, Richard Meran Barsam, editor
New Arts Video, Gregory Battcock, editor
Jack Nicholson, Robert David Crane and Christopher Fryer
Into Film, Laurence Goldstein and Jay Kaufman
The Movies on Your Mind, Harvey R. Greenberg, M.D.
Heroes of Eros, Michael Malone
Women and the Cinema, Karyn Kay and Gerald Peary, editors
Film: A Montage of Theories, Richard Dyer MacCann
King of the B's, Todd McCarthy and Charles Flynn, editors
The American Cinema, Andrew Sarris
The Movie Poster Book, Steve Schapiro and David Chierichetti
Masters of Menace, Ted Sennett
Eisenstein, Norman Swallow
The Birth of the Movies, D. J. Wenden
Expanded Cinema, Gene Youngblood